JAN ZIMMERMAN

ONCE UPON THE FUTURE

A WOMAN'S GUIDE TO TOMORROW'S TECHNOLOGY

Jan Zimmerman is the co-founder and co-owner of Emerson & Stern Associates, a software development firm that focuses on speech and language programming. Her own work is concentrated on the social and political consequences of technology development, including directing a NASA satellite experiment for Narrow Band information transmission for 100 women's organizations.

■ Jan Zimmerman is the editor of *The Technological Woman: Interfacing with Tomorrow*, published by Praeger in 1983.

JAN ZIMMERMAN
ONCE UPON THE FUTURE

A WOMAN'S GUIDE TO TOMORROW'S TECHNOLOGY

PANDORA

New York and London

First published in 1986 by
Pandora Press
(Routledge & Kegan Paul Ltd)

11 New Fetter Lane, London EC4P 4EE

Published in the USA by
Pandora Press
(Routledge & Kegan Paul Inc.)
in association with Methuen Inc.
29 West 35th Street, New York, NY 10001

Set in Times, 10 on 11pt
by Columns of Reading
and printed in the British Isles
by The Guernsey Press Co Ltd
Guernsey, Channel Islands

Library of Congress Cataloging in Publication Data

Zimmerman, Jan.
Once upon the future.
Bibliography: p.
Includes index.
1. Electronic data processing—Vocational guidance.
2. Technology—Vocational guidance.   3. Vocational
guidance for women.   I. Title.
QA76.25.Z56   1986   303.4'83'088042   86-12288

British Library CIP Data also available

ISBN 0-86358-009-2

In loving memory

"Mother Cutter"
Verna H. Fields

Contents

Contents

Contents

Figures

Preface

Once Upon the Future explores the world of technology from a feminist's, a woman's, and a human being's point of view. It is a world at once as foreign as a trip to the moon, and as familiar as the coffeemaker in the kitchen or the digital watch on the wrist. My intent here is neither to extol nor excoriate technology, but to acknowledge the role it plays in all our lives. I want to explore the ways and reasons that women, in particular, suffer under the invisible tyranny of "things" technological; to explain why taking control of technology is so crucial for women trying to take control of their own lives; and to point out how that can be accomplished.

Part I: New Technology, Old Values considers the implications of new technologies, from genetic engineering to videotex information utilities. Not surprisingly, these technologies will further usurp our ability to control our bodies and our environment; they will continue to invade our privacy, transfer societal responsibilities to individuals, alienate us from one another, divide the work we do with our head from the work we do with our hands, and devalue the female content of human life. *Part II: The Invisible Tyranny of Things* establishes the systematic ways this process occurs, from future studies to advertising slogans, from the building of cities to the way we talk about them, from the philosophy of science to the financing of invention. Finally, in *Part III: Tomorrow Is A Woman's Issue*, I describe how we can manipulate the process of technological development to our own advantage by identifying who benefits from the status quo and devising specific strategies to change it.

xiii

If it seems that I am focusing only on the soft, dark underbelly of technology, I am. True, technology has offered us many good things and promises many more: for instance, it may permit the handicapped to function more easily through the use of bioengineering and sensory implants, and may provide genetically engineered cures for sickle cell anemia, Tay-Sachs disease, diabetes, and other illnesses. Machines have reduced the number of excuses available for not hiring women—muscles and might aren't needed to run a fork lift or an electric chain saw. But I must leave to others the writing of paeans to indoor plumbing and elegies to electricity. In this volume, restricted by definition to middle-class experience in contemporary Western civilization, I am playing a deliberate Cassandra to an audience that prefers television to truth.

I play that role from experience: I studied physics as an undergraduate but could not imagine spending my working life with "people like that," and turned to communications without understanding why. I directed a project to connect 100 women's groups using a NASA satellite and was told that the satellite could not be used to discuss issues pertaining to lesbianism or abortion. I have worked as a technical and science writer for newspapers, magazines and defense contractors; I have interviewed computer novices and Nobel Laureates. As a partner and marketing director in a struggling computer software company, I have seen at first hand the corporatizing of technology and the greater importance attached to marketing than to creative ideas, however brilliantly executed. I have met the enemy, but "he is us," as Pogo says, only some of the time.

We need to look outside ourselves to find this particular enemy, most of the time. We are beginning to recognize a con game when we see it. After all, we have been tricked, cheated, swindled and duped before. We've been defrauded by employers, deceived by husbands, and betrayed by government; now we are being deluded by the future—and we're fighting back.

Since this book is written from the gut—and from the heart—it may make you angry. Good. Action comes from anger, and more than anything I would like *Once Upon the Future* to move readers beyond the printed page to action in the real world; if this book instigates nothing but discussion, it will not have achieved much. Therefore, some of the material is deliberately designed to generate dissension; I have provided sources when possible, but it is not possible to reference the imagination. Also, since the world of technology is changing so rapidly, some of my examples may be dated even before this book is on the shelves. But daily life is never out-of-date. Newspapers, television commercials, trips to the bank, the computer system installed at work, the latest kitchen appliance, and other examples in your own life may prove or disprove my points. Observe those examples. Use them. Tangle with them. The list of resource organizations will suggest places to go when you're ready to get involved.

I have written this book for those who expect to be alive in the year 2000 and maybe even for those who don't. You decide: the future is in your hands.

Acknowledgments

A dear friend of mine once told me that she loved reading acknowledgments sections to see how writers "blow kisses" to their friends and colleagues. I have many kisses to blow.

First, to my partner, Sandra E. Hutchins, for helping me structure the book and formulate a method of accomplishing the impossible in a seemingly short time; for taking over many of my responsibilities with our company, 2-Bit™ Software, so I could finish this task; for setting me upright and pointing me in the right direction when I lost my gyroscope; for serving as a walking/talking technical encyclopedia on every topic from encryption to entropy; and for making sure I had twelve hugs a day to grow on.

Over the last several years, many other people have been involved with *Once Upon the Future*. My thanks to researchers Catarina Martinez and Jessie Newburn for their hours in the library with the merest of outlines, trying to read my mind; to bibliographic aides Yoko Arisaka, Emily Fierer, Chris Kehoe and Jennie Saarloos, for putting at infinite number of references into approximately finite order; to Emily Fierer for indexing; to Christine Zmroczek for help with the Appendix; to Anne Geis for handling the burdensome task of obtaining permission for illustrations; to my research associate Eva Klippstrom, to whom fell the less-than-enviable task of checking facts and making sure that what I said was true. She worked long hours under trying conditions, in my kitchen and dining room, in spite of innumerable interruptions and guidance from me that was, at times, haphazard and impatient. I will not soon forget her thrill, however, when she announced that she had just talked to astronaut

Acknowledgments

Kathryn Sullivan; I hope the thrill proved worth the aggravation caused her. Most recently, I owe my thanks to Ann Hargrove and Judi Bugge for proofing galleys and coping with the postal service between the US and UK.

To my readers—Harriet Edwards, Jaime Horwitz, Janis Jenkins, Lauria Peterson, Judy Smith, the late Anna Toth, Susan Trager and Ben Zimmerman—boundless thanks for giving so generously of their knowledge and time, in spite of their own extremely busy lives and, in some cases, personal crises. For their efforts to clarify phrases, correct inaccuracies, and fill in the blanks of my information, I am most grateful; I am not sure, however, where I am going to put the additional basketful of articles they contributed as references. Since among their number I had expertise available in English, sociology, social and environmental psychology, design, architecture, linguistics, computer science, anthropology, appropriate technology, zoology, molecular biology, women's studies, social welfare, public policy planning, law, and common sense, I am deeply indebted to them all, and can only say that all remaining mistakes are mine.

My thanks, too, to architect Leslie Weisman for bringing my work to the attention of Pandora Press. Last, I would like to thank Anonymous for all her inventions, which prove that women can, indeed, take control of technology.

PART I

New Technology, Old Values

[1]
Introduction: the future is history

Once upon a time, as all good fairy tales begin, there was a Land of Do-No-Harm; in this land women controlled all the science and technology. There were plentiful food supplies, clear streams and clean air, safe birth control, shelter and warmth aplenty. Because people had enough to meet their basic needs and all surplus was shared equally, there were no battles for more natural resources, no need to find cheaper supplies of labor or larger markets. As a result, there were no weapons of war and no incessant barrages of propaganda to "prove" who had a better system or a better product. Everybody worked to support the community, and also produced joyful, artistic products. In the fairytale Land of Do-No-Harm, no one ever thought about "progress;" people were content creating beautiful songs and paintings.

Then one day a teenage boy thought it ought to be possible to "Do-No-Harm" more thoroughly than ever before. Probably, he had an Apple. Whether or not he ate it is irrelevant.

The myth of technological determinism

There is no Land of Do-No-Harm, of course, and probably never was. Scenes of pastoral perfection are, regrettably, visions of a false paradise. Since we cannot lose what we never had, we can hardly blame our foremothers for the crazy world we live in now. After all, it was women who developed horticulture and invented tools for cooking, sewing clothes,

3

building shelters, and healing the sick.[1] But how can we explain why we find so few female progeny of those women listed in the ranks of technological inventors today? No law of nature decrees that women cannot or should not be involved in scientific and technological pursuits. Whether or not women perform the experiments, E will continue to equal mc^2 (Einstein's famous equation stating that energy equals mass times the speed of light squared) and the force of gravity will continue to act. Marconi's discovery of radio waves did not predetermine soap operas and game shows, any more than the invention of the internal combustion engine demanded an assembly line.

Once Upon the Future offers an answer to that question, suggesting that technological development, determined by a combination of random events, market forces, and greed, operates to exclude women. Long before the public is aware of new discoveries, a relatively select group of technocrats, acting independently, but sharing a desire to have the future maintain their own preferred values of the past, is able to establish patterns of investment and development. These decision-makers, whose choices are made in their own best interests, pay little, if any, heed to women's needs or the impact of technology on a society broader than their own.

To be sure, it is very difficult to take the technological temperature of an entire society, to assess the various wants and needs of all its many elements, let alone imagine how one invention might ripple through a culture, washing some people ashore on waves of advancement while drowning others. Neither market research nor opinion polling provides an accurate description of reality; both ask people to react to choices presented to them, not to describe new ones. Henry Ford didn't worry about the "horseless carriage" putting blacksmiths out of business any more than the advocates of robotics worry now about automobile assembly line workers losing their jobs. With a collective shoulder shrug they just say, intimations of Social Darwinism deepening their voices, "Well, that's progress. We have to learn to adapt." Unfortunately, the collective hubris of our experiences with pesticides and nuclear fission has not translated into an awareness that there may be some failings in the process—or lack of

4

process—by which technological decisions are made.

There are many who will argue that the idea of making technological choices is, in itself, a kind of hubris, a too-prideful representation of the human role. For these believers in the myth of "technological determinism," there is an internal momentum to discovery; some profoundly unknowable logic that drives the scientific enterprise in sympathetic resonance with human nature; some force that makes unraveling the mysteries of the universe at once irresistible and inevitable. According to this "Star Trek" theory of science, technology happens by default.

Once Upon the Future seeks to defrock this myth, to show that there are very knowable explanations—primarily, but not exclusively, economic—for determining which technologies get developed and which do not; for deciding how expensive they will be (and therefore who will have access to them); what functions they will perform; and what form they will take.

Too many people benefit from the myth of technological determinism for this view to be greeted with open arms. The beneficiaries of technological change gain indirectly by promoting public belief that choices are not possible, while gaining directly from both the process and products that are developed. In particular, without a whisper of conspiracy, each new generation appears to recreate a technological infrastructure that miraculously maintains existing class, race, and gender divisions, thus adding support to the illusion that these divisions are an immutable consequence of nature.

Once Upon the Future explores how this process takes place in the particular case of women. It examines the way technology physically encodes old values of inferiority and subordination into tangible objects; objects, please note, are not easily swayed by persuasive arguments. To elevate woman's place in man's world, we will have to change the very shape and form of material reality. The invisible tyranny of things—from toaster ovens to nuclear reactors—is so crucial in shaping women's roles and expectations that we cannot maintain lasting social change until the physical world is changed too. Social modifications—equal rights, affirmative action programs, team sports—will not suffice. Those modifications can be undone; they are buried when a bulldozer tears up a field; when a new technology, for which women are untrained, moves into the workplace. With one stick of dynamite, technology can tear down the wall of social progress that women have been constructing, brick by brick, for the last twenty years.

Truly, it is dismaying for women to expend tremendous energy to achieve equality today, only to have their efforts undone by a computer tomorrow. It is depressing to see women achieve quotas for employment in job categories that won't exist in five or ten years. It is disheartening to watch women gain access to cable television facilities just as transmisson shifts to satellites. It is demoralizing to watch women gratefully accept technological hand-me-downs while their big brothers buy bigger toys—usually guns—with women's tax money. Most of all, it is discouraging to see women trudging through the mire of the present, when the very images of the future deny their reality and invalidate all the achievements they have struggled so hard to gain.

Crystal balls

The search for the technological source of this persistent and pervasive denial of women's rightful role will take us from anthropology to mythology, from history to media, from politics to science, and back. In contemporary culture, no female Homer sings the story of our lives; instead newscasters tell us "the way it is." Film-makers deftly outline the future in moralistic film fables, while television talk shows bring media personalities into the home for a personal chat. Thus, current history is created not from the shared experience of those we know, so much as from the mediated experience of those we've never met. Similarly, the mass media create an image of the future, not as it will be, for that is impossible, but how it ought to be as an extension of the past.

That image of the future is reflected as surely in the lack of an active female protagonist in *Star Wars* as it is in an advertisement for calculators that pictures a woman's hand holding a "memo-calculator" with the digitally displayed message "Lunch with Nick."[2] That future is described in

Figure 1.1 Service in outer space (*Kate Salley Palmer, Greenville News*)

articles on the city of the future that assume no women will live in them and in a promotional slide for the NASA space shuttle ("the only way to fly"), which portrays a female "chick" stewardess lighting the cigar of a reclining rooster.[3]

These images are prepared and distorted, consciously or otherwise, by an overwhelmingly male workforce in media, advertising, architecture, journalism, aerospace, electronics, business and finance. The images of women they project are the images of a sex-role stereotyped past which is both comforting and comfortable—for men. Women are shown serving and in service to men; they are assumed to fulfill their roles as wife, mother, caretaker and homemaker without digression or dissent. Or, in contrast, women are shown as sex objects, both in the explicitly exploitative poses used to sell advanced technology at trade shows, and in the passive poses that feature women as an attractive accessory for a man to wear, just as he would a new tie.

Far too many articles on the future beg the question of women's role altogether. Articles on genetic and reproductive technology decry the lack of social policy-planning, but never once mention the ultimate consequences of reproductive research on the social and biological roles of women as mothers. Urban planners, proposing grand visions of an architectural future, install the schedules of adult working men, along with steel I-beams, into city layouts that end up creating decades of hardship for working mothers.

The traditional excuses, used to exclude women from public discussion today, offer futurists plenty of opportunities to exclude women from the fantasies of tomorrow as well:[4]

1 It's unnecessarily complicated to include female experience and interests in what is so imprecise and general a formulation of the future.
2 Women's needs are subsumed in the development of systems that meet men's needs.
3 The word "men" is just being used as a convenience—women's concerns have already been included, but aren't separately designated.
4 The future will somehow solve the "woman problem" (and those of minorities and the poor), so these "problem" groups will disappear.

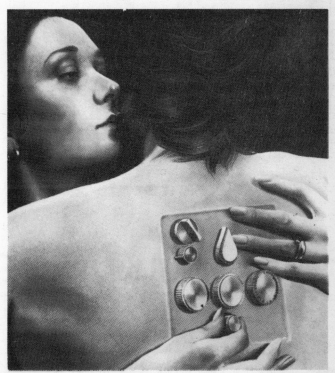
Figure 1.2 Selling sex along with switches (*Electronic Hardware Corporation*)

Unfortunately, neglect by technological planners is rarely benign: it can create severe social, economic and health hazards by developing technology as if tomorrow doesn't matter and women's lives don't count. Such a style of development, which has been described as epidemic in "a civilization committed to the quest for continually improved means to carelessly examined ends,"[5] has already brought us nuclear waste material that's too "hot" to handle, toxic chemical dumps that leak, contagious viruses cloned "by mistake," vaginal cancer caused by DES (diethylstilbesterol), television-addicted children who can't read, valium-addicted adults who can't work, and has started to replace a potentially "troublesome" female secretarial workforce with computers.

We cannot afford to believe in the comforting fairy tale of innocent, value-free technology. Nor can we escape to a delightfully romantic, pre-technical past. If the sharpest critics of technology retreat to the harsh, time- and energy-consuming ethic of self-sufficiency, the remaining population will be even more vulnerable to advertising that promotes the increased consumption of technological products as proof of success. To wish that technology would just "go away" becomes but another means of collaborating in our own oppression. Seeking to destroy the artifacts of industry in a capitalist economy, as the Luddites tried to do with textile equipment in the nineteenth century, will prove to be an equally futile expenditure of personal energy. What then is a woman to do—a woman with two children clinging to her jeans, feet mired in housework, and at least half the burden of household income on her shoulders? How can this woman, for whom tomorrow follows after too little sleep, deal with the relatively distant future of the decade to come? *Once Upon the Future* suggests ways for this woman, and for other women with greater means who empathize with her plight, to question the values embedded in new technologies and to substitute a different set of technologies more consistent with women's needs.

Swimming upstream

The difficulties are enormous. The frontiers of the future will be closed to women, with the excuse that they lack the requisite technical passports for change. The first obstacle to changing women's role in science and technology is their lack of knowledge about math, science, and the processes of technological policy determination. Social conditioning to avoid math and science begins in girls' pre-school years and becomes intense by the time young women are in junior or secondary school.[6] As a result, most women lack the background to undertake science courses in college and are severely under-represented in technical professions. (Women make up less than 6 percent of the engineers in the United States; in the field of electrical engineering, the figure is less than 2 percent;[7] in Britain only 3 percent of professional engineers are women.[8]) When women do manage to run the educational gauntlet they face persistent, sometimes subtle job discrimination regardless of their skills: they are channeled into less glamorous, less remunerative fields; are denied promotion to decision-making positions; and must confront continual attempts by male colleagues and employers to undermine their professional confidence.[9]

Fear places a second burden on the shoulders of women seeking a voice in technical areas: fear of embarrassment, fear of ridicule, fear of being used as a tool by others with greater technological sophistication, fear of inadvertently doing harm to others. Living in a culture of technological hero-worship, where the cult of specialization holds sway, women have too frequently bowed to the opinions of "experts," who extolled the benefits of technology while ignoring its costs. While much of the bloom is now off the technological rose, even today's women, unless they feel technically qualified, are reluctant to challenge "experts," even when issues touch on their own or others' lives.

Third, women, have suffered from the socially and culturally approved policy of fragmenting and isolating women from each other. Thus women are separated blue-collar from white-collar, married from single, mother from childless, technical

11

from secretarial. This practice, reinforced in the media, creates barriers to concerted action which would not otherwise exist, barriers to the articulation of shared goals, to the establishment of joint strategies, and to the formation of coalitions for action. In the particular case of technology, women working as engineers and scientists have been doubly isolated from other women in their working environment and from other aspects of the women's movement. Women's professional organizations have frequently stressed personal advancement in male-dominated fields without connecting their situation to the larger social condition of women, while the women's movement has remained aloof from the stressful reality faced by women in technical fields.

Figure 1.3 How often does a man have to struggle with being a "scientist-man" instead of a "male-scientist"? (*Science for the People, 897 Main Street, Cambridge, Mass. 02139*)

Fourth, every woman working in technology must confront the false personal dichotomy that requires her to claim that she is a "fill-in-the-blank" first and female only second. If women seek acceptance from their male peers, they must eagerly swear their oath of fealty to their profession, over and above all other ties, even to themselves. As every "lady doctor" and "woman engineer" knows, forcing a woman to set these meaningless internal priorities creates an energy-consuming personal conflict that is never demanded of their male colleagues. A woman's refusal to allow the male-defined professional label to take precedence can be used effectively to block her progress in a traditionally male occupation. In her book *Three Guineas*, Virginia Woolf noted this conflict, asking how women can enter the professions and yet remain civilized human beings.[10]

Perhaps the last obstacle is the most damaging of all: the persuasive and ubiquitous myth of women's progress. Companies point eagerly to increased numbers of female employees and newspapers carry feature articles about super-moms with a career, two kids and a gourmet kitchen, implying deceptively that meaningful change has occurred. It is all too easy to overlook US Department of Labor statistics showing that women in 1982 earned only 62 cents for every dollar earned by men, down from 64 cents in 1957,[11] or that women in the UK earn only 71 percent of men's wages in 1981, with "evidence that this relationship is actually deteriorating further".[12] Recognizing that these media myths encourage complacency and reduce dissent is the first step toward recognizing that progress in the future is equally a fairy tale.

Once upon a time

To counterpose these media-transmitted bedtime stories, we must devise and circulate our own mythologies, presenting not only the perceptive analysis of the past that the reclamation of female history provides, but also clear and exciting new views of the future. The National Women's Mailing List and the Women's Computer Literacy Project provide women in the USA with direct access to the computer technology of tomorrow. The National Women's Agenda Satellite Project (now disbanded) sought the use of a NASA satellite to connect 100 women's organizations; the Women's Institute for Freedom of the Press provided nationwide coverage in 1980 of the United Nations Mid-Decade Conference on Women in Copenhagen via satellite. Women's caucuses now exist within many professional societies, including solar energy, mathematics, computer science, physics and electronic engineering. A number of European and North American organizations, such as the Canadian Institute for Research on Public Policy, 9 to 5: The National Association of Working Women, the Swedish Union of Insurance Employees, the Delft Group in the Netherlands, and ISIS in Geneva, Switzerland, are making efforts to alter the negative impacts of office automation on women.

We need to identify our own heroines, and they are there: women astronauts (Sally Ride) and aquanauts (Sylvia Earle), geneticists (Barbara McClintock) and physicists (Vera Kistiakowsky), astronomers (E. Margaret Burbridge) and entrepreneurs (Lore Harp and Carol Ely, who founded Vector Graphic Inc., a computer manufacturing company).

Before we allow ourselves to be deluded by a fairy-tale future in which we will all "live happily ever after" in an electronic castle, heated by nuclear warmth and video-secure against the incursions of reality, we need to take control of tomorrow and rewrite the ending of the story. Surely, the women who rocked the cradle of civilization can forge the crucible of the future.

[2]
Private lives, public choices

At first it may seem that technology is something that happens to other people: space shuttles, laser guns, robots, high-speed computers, electric cars—their relevance to daily life appears so remote that they deserve only the 30-second attention they receive on the nightly news. But technology, in the broad sense of tools or methods used to achieve a practical end, affects nearly every daily activity, from washing dishes to reading at night, from riding a bus to heating a frozen dinner. We take modern technology so much for granted that we have ceased to wonder as we should about its impact on our lives. Out of habit, we carry a dangerous innocence to the new technologies that promise to transform our lives, and then react with astonishment when we have to adjust to the changes they provoke.

In some cases these changes are relatively minor and we accommodate, if not with grace and humor, at least with grudging recognition that change is inevitable. We have managed to accept digital watches without profoundly readjusting our lifestyles; we have integrated mircowave ovens, high-speed trains and quadraphonic sound systems without dramatic shifts in world view. Undoubtedly, we will successfully incorporate cordless phones, digital scales and wristwatch radios. Earlier, major technological innovations of this century—electric power, automobiles, airplanes and television—did, however, transform daily life and forever alter our sense of ourselves, our notions of community and our sense of time and place. We should anticipate that major new innovations, like computers and reproductive engineering, will do the same.

15

Although the pace of technological development seems to have accelerated, we are no more prepared for change than were the past two generations. In particular, we ignore the implications of technological changes in the "private" sphere, even though they may irrevocably reduce our control over the most intimate areas of our lives: birth, quality of life, death. Media reporting on such medical technologies as reproductive engineering, genetic screening, fetal surgery, life prolongation through artificial means and extensive neonatal care tends to focus on their "golly, gee whiz" aspects. Increasingly, the enormous ethical, moral and economic questions these technologies pose is taken out of the hands of the individuals involved and turned over to the medical and legal professions. The bias of these male-dominated professions, both obvious and subtle, poses a particular threat to women's ability to make decisions about their own lives.[1]

A professional discussion

The litany of obvious forms of bias is all too familiar: the historical under-representation of women in medicine and law until the 1970s, when US government policies required professional schools to admit women according to their abilities (women now make up 23-35 percent of those programs in the US)—in the UK approximately 23 percent of the medical profession and only 14 percent of the legal profession are women; the patronizing tone in which women are described, from drug-industry advertisements promoting tranquilizers for the "smiling volunteer . . . still taking care of her home and family . . . who is so overanxious to appear good and dependable,"[2] to judges who say, "Stand up and turn around honey. . . . Isn't it hard to believe this pretty little lady is an attorney general?"[3] Institutional hostility toward women abounds, from assumptions that rape is a normal reaction when a woman dresses provocatively,[4] to the appalling insensitivity of medical classes and textbooks discussing the impact of breast surgery.[5] The list of biases could go on and on, but for the need to consider the more subtle ways in which the medical and legal professions exploit women by

16

cultivating emotional dependency and denying them control over their own lives.

Historically speaking, members of these professions cannot be trusted to make decisions in the best interests of their patients or clients. For instance, when the medical profession in the US first wrested control over childbirth from midwives in the nineteenth century, cases of puerperal fever, caused by dirty hands and instruments, rose. By the 1920s episiotomy, the surgical enlargement of the vagina during childbirth, became common practice whether or not it was necessary, and women were placed on uncomfortable, stirruped tables during labor and delivery because that position was more convenient for their male doctors. By the late 1970s fetal monitoring became routine, again because of convenience, and the number of Caesarean sections in the United States escalated to 25 percent—40 percent of all births in some hospitals. Under challenge from natural childbirth, home birth and women's rights advocates, some US states have once again allowed nurse-midwives to practice (albeit under a physician's supervision), hospitals have established home-like birthing suites, and Lamaze classes have become popular. The time frame was slightly different in the UK and Europe, but the net result of transferring control over birth from midwives to doctors has been the same.

The law offers no historical solace either. "The law," until the last few decades, prevented women from owning property in their own names, condoned wife-beating, prohibited women from obtaining patents, and permitted the exclusion of women from educational institutions, some workplaces, and the voting booth. (Without the organized political pressure of the women's movement—and the recently increased number of sympathetic women lawyers—these changes still would not have been made.) In the most subtle of all forms of disrimination, the law misrepresents a male-defined codification of social ethics as an expression of collective will. Yet Carol Gilligan, in her book *In a Different Voice*, argues eloquently and conclusively that most women have a totally different code for making ethical decisions—one based on the real impacts of an event on the parties involved, rather than on abstract notions of justice; one that values personal

17

relationships over individual rights.[6]

In evaluating new technologies we must acknowledge the vested self-interest of the professions in maintaining their status. We must recognize that they gain power from the demands of the middle class for prestigious career opportunities on one hand, and for readily available "expert" advice on the other.[7] We must acknowledge that the professions, on the whole, place a premium upon a very different definition of the moral "good" than women do. Since the complexity of modern society encourages us to rely only on trained "specialists" to frame the questions, set the priorities, and evaluate the results, women, who are vastly under-represented in technical professions, do not have the necessary opportunity to promote technologies that would reflect their self-interest or extend their options. The resulting conflicts over control of technology are, perhaps, most pressing and personal where reproductive issues are involved.

Reproductive engineering: redefining parenthood

In the martial arts, "arm's length" is defined as the territory that must always be protected. In the sense of protecting bodily territory, any technology that impinges on a woman's control over her own body is suspect. While women, as well as men, must struggle with medical technologies that affect the length and quality of life, they must also deal with an even more private, interior space—the womb. The centrality of reproduction to the definition of women's role in society has been analyzed at various times from biological, mythic, historical, social and psychological perspectives; now it is time to consider it from a technological one.[8]

In the long view, early struggles over access to birth control and more recent ones over abortion rights may appear as mear skirmishes in a reproductive war. Perhaps because birth is one area impossible for men to control totally, they, as a gender, have sought throughout history to exert their authority over as much of the process as possible. The attack on this female domain, exacerbated in a patriarchal society that transferred property to the first-born son (primogeniture), arises also from the biological difficulty of a father knowing his own child (and vice versa). "Who am I?" is, after all, a question of male identity in literature and mythology, from Homer's *Odyssey* to Saul Bellow's *Herzog* (the female equivalent is "How do I fit in?").

New technologies of engineered conception will ultimately eliminate paternal uncertainty by fertilizing a designated egg *in vitro* (in glass) with a designated sperm and implanting the designated embryo into a designated womb. Future battles will rage over the territories of artificial insemination, surrogate motherhood, embryo transfer, and cloning. A brief look at each of these will show how women's interests are at stake.

Artificial insemination, implanting sperm near a woman's cervix, with anything from a turkey baster to a syringe, has been done in a variety of settings for nearly 200 years. Originally performed as a means for a woman to bear a child even if her husband was not fertile, it recently has become popular with single women and lesbian couples desiring a child. It can also be combined with a technique for separating male sperm from female sperm to increase the odds of conceiving a male child. (Since first-born children have an advantage in achieving success, a society in which all the first-born children are male would be even more inequitable.)

As a result of advances in cryogenics and genetic screening, categorized sperm can be stored for long periods of time, thus making sperm banks possible. US banks, which usually operate for profit, pay donors $20-$35 for their contribution and charge recipients $135-$195 per sample. (Several tries are often necessary before a woman becomes pregnant.) Sperm banks are not required to keep accurate records, to provide the biological father's name for a birth certificate, or to meet any other legal conditions. In fact, many banks deliberately mix sperm from several donors to "hide" the identity of the father, even though an accurate medical history and genetic matching for organ transplant may be crucial for the offspring's well-being. Only one state (Oregon) even requires screening to eliminate sperm with genetic defects or from donors with venereal diseases. Even though a woman may get a child with the hair or eye color she requests, both she and her offspring are at serious risk.[9]

New technology, old values

The British Pregnancy Advisory Service, which is the only organizational sperm bank in the UK, charges women £50 for an initial visit and £50 per month for insemination and sperm; sperm donors receive £7 for their "contribution". Like US sperm banks, BPAS protects the anonymity of the sperm donors, but allows recipients to select for physical characteristics. However, BPAS requires women to have their partner's consent to prevent recrimination, which is not required in the United States. Insemination is available on the National Health Service in some areas, but is very difficult to obtain.

In a virulent throwback to pre-Renaissance medicine, the Repository for Germinal Choice in Escondido, California, claims to stock only the sperm of Nobel Laureates, casually ignoring potential mothers' intelligence or medical health. "We're not so critical of the [sperm] recipient as of the donor," says founder Robert Graham.[10]

Since we have known for over 300 years that Aristotle was wrong (women's contribution to conception is *not* insignificant), it is hard to see this sperm bank as a technological advance promoting women's interests. Yet legislators seem reluctant to supervise such businesses, perhaps because they sympathize with couples who seek artificial insemination in an embarrassed conspiracy to hide a husband's infertility, for fear infertility might imply impotence as well. This sympathy extends to issuing phony birth certificates showing the husband's name, rather than the biological father's, making a step-parent adoption unnecessary and covering up any legal trail that might give a child a clue to its genetic origins. As a result, a great shroud of secrecy surrounds the genetic inheritance of the "sperm donor baby," even though an enlightened adoption community has begun to challenge similar policies in ordinary adoption cases.

Artificial insemination remains almost exclusively under the control of doctors, again a predominantly male club. Doctors determine who is allowed to reproduce this way and can at whim deny artificial insemination to single women, lesbians, or married women who don't have their husband's consent. Only one woman-controlled facility in the world, the Feminist Women's Health Center, a full-service, self-help clinic in Oakland, California, operates its own sperm bank so that women can take control of the entire procedure.[11]

When compared to the legislative control exerted over the parallel situation of arranged surrogate motherhood, the discrimination appears more bold. A surrogate mother, artificially inseminated to fertilize her own egg, carries the resulting fetus to term, at which point the child is transferred to the contracting couple. (Doctors have allowed only married, heterosexual couples access to this method, although there is no medical reason why a single, infertile woman, a single man, or a homosexual couple couldn't contract a surrogate mother for the same "service.") Unlike the situation with artificial insemination, surrogate parent organizations operate under varying degrees of legal scrutiny. The baby is registered under the birth mother's name; it must be formally adopted by the step-mother; reputable groups generally insist that the adopting couple and the surrogate mother meet. (Commercial surrogate motherhood is currently illegal in the UK, but goes on all the same.)

In most cases, the contracting couple pays a fee of up to $25,000, of which $15,000 goes for legal, psychological and medical costs and $10,000 goes to the surrogate mother. Since the cost, which is not covered by insurance companies, is prohibitive, access to this means of parenthood is available only to a wealthy few. Most surrogate mothers carry the baby for the money, although many also cite altruistic feelings as part of their willingness to participate.[12] The potential thus exists to create a low-income class of women who serve as "paid wombs," in an extension of the "wet nurse" tradition of the Middle Ages and later.

There are many other difficulties with the terms of these contracts, particularly regarding the right of a couple to refuse a retarded or birth-damaged child, the right of the surrogate mother to refuse amniocentesis or abortion, or to refuse to give up the child after birth, and her right to additional payment as a result of damage to her physical health during pregnancy.

Neither eggs nor sperm are "donated" in the "test tube" baby technique (*in vitro* fertilization). Eggs are removed from the woman's ovary during a surgical procedure called a laparoscopy, fertilized with sperm in a glass Petri dish, and then re-implanted in the woman's womb for pregnancy. Although there is no medical reason that the egg and sperm must come from a husband and wife pair (any combination of egg and sperm will do), doctors have restricted this procedure to married couples. The average $4000 cost per implantation (several may be needed) is outside normal insurance coverage, creating *de facto* class and possibly racial segregation; to date only white women have had test tube babies. The first test tube baby, Louise Brown, was born in Britain in 1978 and so many more have been born since that it is no longer "news."[13]

Embryo transfer techniques represent the latest "advances" in reproductive engineering. In one method, a woman donates an unfertilized egg for *in vitro* fertilization and the resulting embryo is implanted in another woman's womb for development; the first "donor egg" baby was born in November 1983 at Monash University in Melbourne, Australia. In another variation, a woman is artificially inseminated, fertilization occurs within her uterus, and the embryo is washed out for implantation in a different woman. In January 1984 doctors at Harbor/UCLA Medical Center in Torrance, California, announced the first baby born through this process;[14] the medical team is trying to patent the process and start a profit-making embryo transfer business. Both these procedures again assume that an unrelated woman will donate the egg, that sperm will be provided by the contracting husband, and that the contracting wife will carry the embryo for the duration of the pregnancy. In such cases, serious questions could arise over the primacy of the gestational versus the genetic mother's rights and over who would be legally and financially responsible for a child born with birth defects. These questions became more than theoretical in 1984: an IVF candidate couple died, leaving fertilized embryos in storage in Melbourne, giving rise to questions about the right to life and inheritance of frozen embryos.

Since a surrogate mother could accept an embryo fertilized either *in vitro* or in another woman, it is possible now to rationalize the phases of reproduction, just as assembly lines break down manufacturing jobs into separate tasks: one woman could supply the egg, another could carry the pregnancy to term, and yet a third could be responsible for rearing the child, with other caretakers supplementing her efforts. The phrase "reproduction of the labor force" could take on a very different meaning in the future!

The ultimate method for controlling parenthood would be cloning, where the genetic material for the child comes from the *body cell* of any one adult. This has not yet occurred with human cells, but it has been tried with animal cells. The clone would share identical genetic material (and therefore gender) with its one parent, just as identical twins share the same genetic composition, but would still be an individual in its own right. While this would enable a man literally to produce a son in his own image (or a woman a daughter), women would still be needed as "warm wombs" for at least a few months of pregnancy.

The most troublesome aspect of these technologies is that they are being investigated and/or implemented with minimal public dialog of any kind, and even less input specifically from women. The Warnock Report, commissioned by the UK government and published in 1984, gave the results of a public hearing about the wisdom of new reproductive technologies, but predictably had little input from ordinary women and paid little attention to long-term consequences for them. No caucus except the low-profile Feminist International Network on New Reproductive Engineering Technologies (FINNRET) is dealing with the potential impact of these technologies on every woman's right to assess risks for herself and to decide when, how, or whom to conceive; on financially discriminatory access to alternative means of conception as well as contraception; on fetal "rights" versus female rights. While women fight a rearguard, defensive action on abortion, right-to-life groups could co-opt the "right-to-birth" issue in such a way that low-income women are economically coerced into childbearing as surrogate mothers, even while other low-income women are denied access to technological solutions for their own infertility.

In 1981 Planned Parenthood, a US nationwide family planning organization, had to withdraw its request to have the Board of Supervisors in San Diego County, California, approve the organization's application for a federal grant to offer fertility clinic services to about fifty indigent couples.

Supervisor Roger Hedgecock, who later became mayor of San Diego, contended "that there are 'too many people' in the world already, without finding 'some poor people who may have problems having babies and [assisting] them to do that.' "[15]

Reproductive engineering, a technology with incalculable consequences for women, remains both "private" and privatized. Under these conditions, women do not control the process of giving birth; medical researchers do. Unlike abortion, a personal decision that generates vociferous public debate, these forms of mediated conception, which distance the female person from the decisions being made, provoke very little discussion. Reporters, fascinated by the techniques used to conceive test tube and donor egg babies, rarely raise the issues of access and cost, or explore the implications of these developments. Without greater awareness on the part of women, medical professionals will be left, by default, to control the research; the question about whether reproductive engineering is wise will never be answered by those who must cope with the consequences.

Privacy: a peripheral issue?

In *1984* George Orwell warned about worldwide totalitarianism enforced by the omnipotent technologies of Big Brother.[16] News commentators focus on whether or not his gloomy predictions have come true literally, without considering how well laissez-faire capitalism has succeeded in implementing some of the very same technologies under a different guise. Although these privacy-invading technologies affect both women and men, they are included here as cautionary tales of how a "private" technology can sneak in under the tent, without causing any public commotion. Even leaving aside the relatively familiar abuse of personal information stored in computer databases, we can come up with a chilling imitation of an Orwellian future.

While Orwell wrote about two-way televisions used to spy on everyone, and the press remains preoccupied with Russians encouraging neighbors to spy on each other, cable television networks have gone quietly about their business of keeping records, apparently with the tacit consent of their viewers. For instance, a theater owner arrested for showing a pornographic film in Columbus, Ohio, supoenaed the records of QUBE, a two-way cable system owned by Warner/Amex, to prove that the film met legally acceptable "community standards" because a number of prominent residents had watched the same movie over cable. (The judge forced the cable company to release the numbers, but not names, of viewers; QUBE had both.)[17]

The same cable company has been involved in a market research experiment to evaluate which commercials effectively generate purchases. Cable customers who agree to participate receive an identification card that indicates which of several alternative commercials for the same product they have seen. A light scanner at the supermarket check-out counter correlates their ID card with their purchases by reading the Zebra or bar code (Universal Product Code) on each item. Advertisers then match consumption patterns to commercials, ostensibly resulting in more cost-effective advertising.[18] It sounds innocent enough, but the same technique of targeting particular information to demographically preselected segments of the viewing audience can be used to target news programs or political campaign spots as well. Without being aware of it, viewers could receive different campaign spots or news programs; no channel flipping or "tuning in" to a particular show would be necessary. In addition, computer devices that flash subliminal messages or whisper them below conscious hearing range, from "Buy Heineken Beer" to "Vote Republican," can be coupled to the screen image.

Or consider the technological horrors people inflict on themselves in the name of security. They install photoelectric burglar alarms sensitive to motion, flashing-light alarms triggered by noise, voice-activated locks and keys, radio frequency-controlled security gates, and video surveillance cameras that monitor legitimate activities as well as illegitimate ones. Terrified by television violence and newspaper reports of crime, people turn themselves into prisoners in the hope of protecting their lives and their possessions. Ironically, George Gerbner's studies at the Annenberg School of

Communications at the University of Pennsylvania have shown that people's expectation of becoming a crime victim is much greater than its actual likelihood.[19]

What better way to control a society than to have all the law-abiding citizens lock themselves in, while the thieves and thugs, and police and intelligence agencies, are free on the street! One corollary effect is that we become so accustomed to the presence of surveillance technologies that we are not as outraged as we should be by government-ordered wiretaps, airport metal detectors, or TV cameras placed on public streets "to deter crime."[20] Another is that we dismiss potent approaches like "Neighbourhood Watch" groups (a local community action group or block club technique for crime prevention) or feminist drives to "Take Back the Night" (marches and demonstrations to make the streets safe for women), both of which enhance a sense of community interdependence, in favor of a more expensive, more impersonal, individually purchased "technological fix."

The potential for even greater abuse of privacy lies in computer communications links for personal banking, paying bills, shopping, reading electronic publications, or "chatting." Since these transactions can be monitored as they occur, it will be possible to amass a far more detailed picture of every individual's life than ever before.[21] Rest assured that banks and utility companies will seek to maintain "secure" links to prevent loss of funds from their accounts, but who will pay for the effort to secure our records from interlopers? Yet we rush blithely in where Orwell feared to tread, unwittingly sacrificing privacy for convenience.

These are not examples of technology gone awry; that is their horror. They are examples of technology eagerly embraced by a too-casual public, convinced that "free choice" among consumption activities is the true meaning of "life, liberty, and the pursuit of happiness." As a consequence, we face the division of society into new classes, whose membership will be defined by who is observed and who is not, who has privacy and who does not; who imposes criteria and upon whom they are imposed. Many more people will then share the fates of the poor, the institutionalized and the elderly, whose dependency on welfare checks, psychiatric hospitals and old-age homes leaves them vulnerable to critical and constant surveillance of their behavior.

When technologies like security and reproductive engineering are dressed in the silken folds of "individual rights," we must learn to be wary. The Emperor of New Technology might be wearing synthetics instead of silk, or he might not be dressed at all.

[3]

The domesticated city

While technology, on the one hand, exposes private decisions to public scrutiny, on the other hand it helps transfer social responsibilities from the larger political realm to the private home—and to the woman who runs it. The nature of computer data entry and electronics assembly piecework is used to justify why women should be able to care for children while working at home; the existence of labor-saving household appliances is used to explain why women should be able to assume almost all domestic tasks. The primary result of bringing more technology into the home is that women end up doing ever more work for ever less pay.

Caretaking institutions, from mental hospitals to reform schools, that have been the responsibility of the state are now being turned over, in effect, to churches, private charities, commercial enterprises, professionals, and families. Churches run soup kitchens; private charities provide shelters for the homeless and for battered women; profit-making businesses build and operate jails and hospitals; professionals run drug and alcohol abuse clinics; and families become halfway houses for mentally ill patients released from state institutions. The transfer of responsibilities, superficially caused by budget cuts, is actually a continuation of a long historical decline in the provision by society of public welfare.[1] The expanded social services offered between the 1930s and the 1960s were merely an anomaly.

Perhaps the most explicit recognition of a social obligation to provide a source of community economic support was the existence of commonly owned grazing lands (the "commons") in English and European villages in the late Middle Ages. The commons, regrettably, began to disappear during the Renaissance, with the growth of a cash economy and the rise of capitalism. (Although the concept left a legacy in public recreational parks, these, too, are becoming commercialized and privatized through membership-only gyms, golf courses, tennis courts and swimming clubs.) The Elizabethan poor laws of the early seventeenth century did acknowledge some limited parish responsibility for public welfare, but by the nineteenth century the most important function of the poorhouses and workhouses created under their aegis was to provide a means of social control. It took another hundred years and a severe economic depression for the state to assume such additional obligations as welfare payments, unemployment benefits, disability insurance, social security for the elderly, and in the United States food stamps and insurance for the medically indigent, in the UK the National Health Service. These reformist measures were meant, however, to head off any truly revolutionary changes in the economic system, not to admit responsibility for public support.

Now, these "safety nets," too, are reverting to private forms ("plan for your old age with an IRA or KEOGH retirement plan"), as conservative political administrations slash the budgets of the "welfare state," both to reduce the number of recipients and to return to the nostalgic past of unfettered capitalism. Other caretaking functions, like day care for children of working mothers, adult day care for the dependent segment of the senior population, and rehabilitative services for the physically or mentally handicapped, are being reinterpreted as chores that should be handled in a "loving family atmosphere"—and that means women—mothers, grandmothers, daughters or wives—at home. Very, very rarely have men undertaken such unpaid, labor-intensive activities.

Bringing the city back home

With this twist of the prism, the disadvantages of tele-commuting—working by computer from the home—suddenly appear. Telecommuting, lauded as a means of saving gasoline and saving time, encourages the transmutation of societal obligations into women's obligations, while simultaneously serving the ends of the pro-family movement, which seeks to re-create the nuclear family. With electronic homework, the elderly can become self-supporting and "more desirable to have around," says a National Science Fondation Report.[2] With electronic homework, says futurist Alvin Toffler, citing an Institute for the Future prediction, "married secretaries caring for small children at home [can] continue to work."[3] (Nowhere is there any mention of telecommuting fathers caring for small children or the elderly.)

The values behind these images are trebly discriminatory. First, the assumption that women should be the ones to stay home and care for the young, the old and the infirm reinforces socialization patterns that link gender and nurturance. Second, the statement implies that neither women's worklife nor their caretaking function is important enough to demand full-time attention. (A woman cannot concentrate on meaningful work with an infant on her lap. Nor can a woman working on a computer at home keep a toddler away from the stove or read to an elderly parent; day care is still essential.) And third, it presumes that women will continue to hold routine, low-paying data entry jobs, thus completing the vicious circle that makes those jobs the only ones caretaking mothers can hold. These assumptions run counter to two recent social changes: women's surge into the labor force (women composed nearly 45 percent of the US and over 40 percent of the UK workforce in 1983, and contributed to the financial support of 97 percent of all US families and 88 percent of British ones); and the increasing variety of family forms (less than 7 percent of American households in 1980 were composed of the traditional homemaker Mom, breadwinner Dad, two or more kids, and a dog; in the UK the figure is about 11 percent.[4] By reinforcing these outdated assumptions, however, electronic homework is manipulated to re-create the past.

Telecommuting promises two very different types of work experiences for those at the upper and lower ends of the occupational scale: data entry clerks and secretaries will handle routine tasks under continuous computer scrutiny of their performance and hours, while professionals will have discretionary working hours and unrestricted freedom to use the computer for personal tasks, such as home accounting and database access.[5] As long as job segregation persists (women make up more than 95 percent of all secretaries and data entry personnel in the US, but less than 30 percent of all managers and administrators[6]), telecommuting will be much less tantalizing for women than it is for men in managerial positions, to whom it offers greater independence.

For immigrant, sometimes undocumented, Third World women, who constitute the majority of electronics assemblers, computer homework has a different meaning. Those minimally skilled Asian women and Latinas who hope to earn a living in high-tech environments like "Silicon Valley" in California find themselves packing circuit boards on a piecework basis in their kitchens and garages, often pressing their children into service, even if dangerous chemicals are involved. Manufacturers, who generally hire subcontractors to manage such "electronics sweatshops," appreciate this system: they can pay below minimum wages, eliminate benefits, and avoid occupational health and safety regulations. Labor contractors frequently collect kickbacks from the women, who are grateful for the work, willing to accept overhead costs as their own, and too terrified of immigration authorities to report abuses.[7]

If these obviously exploitative conditions could be eliminated, home-based assembly work *could* be of real benefit. Since low-paid assembly workers often cannot afford day care, second cars, or housing near their jobs, homework offers these women a chance to reduce the cost and time of commuting long distances by public transit, and an escape from hostile, often racially discriminatory work environments. Because they do not address those needs, the efforts of some labor unions to outlaw homework meet with resistance from female workers.[8]

There are alternatives that would both avoid the abuses of piecework practices and meet justifiable labor union concerns. Unions, for instance, could act as hiring halls, monitoring pay scales to assure that fair wages and benefits are paid. Or assembly workers could form collectives to establish decentralized, neighborhood-based, mini-worksites, with day care on the premises and occupational safety and health conditions regulated. Electronics assembly or computer workstation sites

31

could be shared by people working for many different companies. As independent contractors, these women could set their own hours, work without supervision, and elect their own facilities coordinator.

A matter of survival

Household technology has also encouraged the shift of domestic burdens from collective shoulders to those of the individual woman in the individual home. In extended family cultures of the past, many routine tasks, such as gathering food and wood, cooking, shelter construction and laundry were shared. (These jobs were still gender-defined, but not every woman had to do every job.) American Indian women, for example, were responsible for providing their tribes with baskets, pottery, cooking utensils, preserved food, woven textiles, sewn-leather garments and shoes, depending on the climate and the resources available. Women of the Plains tribes constructed and transported tepees; women of the southwest Indian tribes built all the ovens and hearths in their pueblos. Shared labor and specialization of tasks marked the lives of Black slavewomen on southern plantations and characterized the nineteenth-century pioneer lifestyle, which elevated collective survival technologies into social events: sewing parties, roof-raisings and harvesting activities.

With increased urbanization, survival tasks among white, non-immigrant families became more household-centered. Middle- and upper-class homes at the turn of the century required numerous servants to handle the labor-intensive chores of washing clothes, building wood and coal fires, emptying chamberpots, filling kerosene lanterns, carrying water, beating rugs and preparing food. Like domestic workers today, lower-class immigrant women had to maintain both their own and others' homes. The labor of servants was supplemented by numerous service-based small businesses, including tailors, washerwomen, seamstresses, shoe repairers and knife-sharpeners, deliverers of milk, ice, fuel, groceries and vegetables, and itinerant peddlers, gardeners and handymen.

Technological developments in the first few decades of the twentieth century encouraged a shift to self-sufficient, individually run households in the US by supplying natural resources directly to the home. Indoor plumbing, water systems, gas and electrical utilities, and the development of the oil furnace dramatically reduced dependence on outside suppliers. The invention of large appliances (refrigerators, gas and electrical ovens, washing machines, wringers, dryers) and small ones (sewing machines, blenders, vacuum cleaners) enabled a single worker to maintain a household that once demanded the labor of many hands. New household technologies, plus a servant "crisis" induced by US immigration restrictions in the 1920s and the availability of jobs more appealing than domestic labor after World War I, thus contributed to the privatization of housework. As a result of these events, the paid labor of female servants (or the shared labor of many hands) was supplanted by the unpaid labor of the individual wife.[9]

The alternative to privatizing housework would have been to expand market services to support household functions. However, urban sprawl, encouraged by the invention of the automobile, deterred the expansion of services delivered to the home. Concomitantly, the domestic science movement, which extended the principles of scientific management to the home through the work of such writers as Christine Frederick and Lillian Gilbreth, discouraged the establishment of the communal housekeeping services suggested by utopian and socialist feminists. Domestic science "proved" that a woman working alone, if she was efficient, could manage a home.

Ironically, although many home technologies reduced the physical labor involved in servicing the household, they did not decrease the amount of time required. Numerous studies have shown that women today spend the same amount of time on housework as their grandmothers did; only the content of the work has changed.[10] Today's woman, even when she works outside the home, spends more time in purchasing, transporting, parenting, supervising, planning, and managing repair and maintenance than her predecessor did.

Rising standards of childcare and domestic performance help maintain women's burden; a "good mother" now

(a)

(b)

(c)

(d)

chauffeurs her children to music lessons, Scouts and dance class, and a "good wife" provides gourmet meals to entertain business associates. What used to be expected only of the wealthy woman, who had paid help, is now expected of the ordinary, middle-class woman who works outside the home as well. Status- or energy-conscious consumers are further expected to purchase silks and cottons, which demand ironing that permanent press fabrics do not, and to furnish their homes with wood, leather and tile products, rather than plastics, nylon, vinyl or Formica. "Natural goods" may take less chemical energy to produce, but women must spend much more female energy to maintain them.

Figure 3.1   Artist Harriete Estel Berman has created "The Family of Appliances You Can Believe In." Her satirical works and their accompanying advertisements mock both the anachronism of women's traditional roles in contemporary society and the possibility of consumer goods increasing personal leisure.
(**a**) *Toast to the Bride*   Quality is timeless and this shiny nickel-plated toaster with its elegant black trim will undoubtedly become the standard by which others are judged. The toaster opens to reveal a quilted satin interior with the Bride enthroned on a pedestal of real Wonder Bread, completely saturated with polyester resin. *It should last a lifetime! (Harriete Estel Berman)*
(**b**) *Marry Me For My Hobart*   Whatever dream you whip up, this mixer is custom-designed to accommodate your individual needs. Clean, traditional styling, a smooth and lustrous finish and a 14K gold ring will ensure everlasting pride and pleasure. *Kitchen tried—kitchen tested (Harriete Estel Berman)*
(**c**) *Womanizer, Kitchen Queen*   Custom-designed to suit the needs of every busy homemaker, this innovative blender features a ten-button panel: love, honor, obey, cherish, mix, blend, stir, cream, spread, and bear. Complement your Harvest Gold color scheme with a real crown on the lid. Wind up the music box to "Wish Upon a A Star" and watch the ballerina dance. *You must see this model to fully appreciate its attractiveness and beauty (Harriete Estel Berman)*
(**d**) *Misstress of the Home: Bound to Modern Convenience*   This revolutionary vacuum lets you spend less time on housework, and will give years of trouble-free service. Do your chores in style with this eye-catching appliance designed to take your breath away. *Beats as it sweeps as it cleans (Harriete Estel Berman)*

Nor does technology encourage men to handle more duties around the house. In spite of the women's movement and new technology, women in the US continue to provide 80-95 percent of household maintenance services.[11] In some cases, technology actually increases women's share of the chores: more women take out the garbage when garbage disposals (waste disposal units) reduce the weight of trash cans; more women do the dishes when dishwashers are available; and numerous small appliances actually make more work for women than they save.

Since rising transportation costs and increasing distances have shifted the burden of travel from the producer to the consumer, women now spend countless hours traveling from dry cleaner to supermarket, shoe repair to car repair, greengrocer to pizza parlor. The outdated assumption that women have "free time" to spend on such consumption activities is contradicted by the frantic schedules of working mothers, for whom "free time" is an unheard-of luxury. The recent growth of direct mail, catalog shopping is an inadequate response to this new reality. Daily-use goods are not available; catalogs still take time to read; and items like clothes and shoes are best purchased in person.

The very design of homes built after World War II makes women's work more difficult; male architects, after all, have little experience of what really goes on in the kitchen or around the house. New kitchens, unlike Great-grandmother's, rarely offer enough space for several people to work at once. Since kitchens are often cut off from other living spaces (so the static from the blender won't disrupt the television show . . .), the amount of work involved in meal preparation and clean-up becomes invisible: out of sight, out of mind. The nearby family room or lounge, which now has the hearth, serves as the focus of the home for everyone except mother, who has no space but the kitchen to call her own.[12] The back-breaking design of bathtubs makes it difficult to bathe children; lack of adequate storage space wastes time reshuffling items; plush wall-to-wall carpets can't be sent out for cleaning. Ah, for inventor Frances GABe's self-cleaning house! In GABe's house, dishes are washed in the cupboard, clothes are cleaned in the closets, and the rest of the house sparkles after a humid misting and blow dry![13]

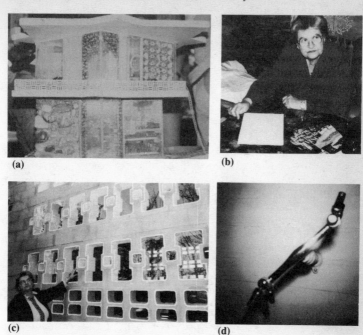

Figure 3.2 Frances GABe's innovative self-cleaning house would offer a technological alternative to time-consuming housework. Clockwise from upper right:
(a) A model of the self-cleaning house
(b) Frances sits at a desk sealed with one of her inventions, a no-bother top to keep out moisture while the house is cleaned
(c) Window-wall building blocks have 7 inches of dead air insulation for temperature control
(d) The general room-washing apparatus is the heart of the GABe self-cleaning house. Each unit will spray a warm mist under controlled pressure to clean a 45 × 50 foot area and then blow warm, pressurized air to dry it (*Frances GABe*)

Perhaps the ultimate ironic comment on the irrelevance of current technology to women's lives comes from a radio commercial for Atari computers. While the male announcer recites a litany of what the computer can do ("You can learn a new language, link up to a world of information by phone . . .

or take your best shot playing Missile Command"), a woman's voice interrupts, "Now . . . does it clean up?"[14]

The myth of self-sufficiency

There are some who decry energy-consuming new technology and argue that we must return to an era of self-sufficiency through alternative technology. Obviously, there never really was such an era: family networks, market services, servants and community support structures made it possible for people to survive without energy-consuming technologies. To try to do so now would demand not only the use of alternative, renewable energy resources, which is both feasible and attractive, but also the development of totally different household technologies and social structures, neither of which is likely.

Unfortunately, most of those who support "appropriate technologies" (defined as decentralized, small-scale, low-cost, and low in fossil fuel consumption) would substitute women's energy for oil.[15] To require women to stay at home to bake bread, grow vegetables, preserve fruit or sew insulating curtains as a means of survival is absurd. Yet those who criticize microwave ovens or condemn clothes dryers rarely volunteer to undertake the responsibility of making dinner or hanging clothes on the line for a family of five. Nuclear power advocates may be supporting a hazardous and needless technology, but they have an effective, if erroneous, comeback when they imply a shortage of electrical power in an ad that reads, "Try telling the little lady she'll have to start washing by hand."[16]

For a woman to hold down two full-time jobs, one in the paid workplace and one at home, such energy-consuming devices as an automobile are absolutely essential. Margaret McCormack of the California Office of Appropriate Technology put the conflict well:[17]

I recall watching college students bury a gas guzzling car on Earth Day '70 [and] thinking that they had never raced in such a car to an emergency ward on the other side of town

38

at 3 a.m. with one feverish baby in the front seat and its healthy sibling sleeping in the back. Nor did they have the harried daily routines of driving miles in one direction to the only available childcare center, miles in another direction to get to work, back to the center before it closed, and off in yet another direction to pick up some food for dinner. Nor had they probably ever tried using bicycles to shop or do laundry with two kids in tow.

To be sure, there are questions about the necessity of digital dishwashers or the planned obsolescence of toasters and TVs, but we must consider whether the time-consuming alternative of household self-sufficiency without electrical power would be worth its cost in womanpower. Total self-sufficiency would make community unnecessary and social infrastructure meaningless. Perhaps it is not so bad, then, to have household appliances that break down, as long as we can share the responsibility of waiting at home for the repair service to come and have the money to pay them.

Technology has tended to isolate us in our homes, to alienate us from one another, to substitute vicarious experience for direct knowledge, and to reduce opportunities for face-to-face communication. It has encouraged the fragmentation of the extended family into multiple, isolated ones and supported the physical atomization of the community into so many separate, single-family homes. We have lost community to gain a false sense of independence and forfeited human contact out of fear of others. What we need to understand is why.

As with other technologies, we need to consider who benefits from privatized household tasks. Not women, certainly, since time-consuming household burdens rest upon their shoulders. Men gain, to a great degree, since they benefit from having a resident domestic caretaker meet their personal needs and relieve them of distasteful but essential chores, from cleaning the toilet to changing diapers and emptying the fridge of leftovers. Convenience is certainly one reason men prefer private services to public or market ones. Communal, public or market services have disadvantages: they must be shared, contracted, negotiated, acquired; they rarely provide exactly what someone needs exactly when it is needed or wanted.

Cost, however, is the greatest attraction. Women's labor in the home is unpaid, while public services are paid with taxes, and market ones with cash. When their personal income increases, people seek costly market services as a sign of status, from live-in maids, housekeepers, chauffeurs and nannies, to expensive restaurant meals and hand-tailored clothing. Unpaid, private labor by a woman in the home allows a middle-class man to delude himself into believing that he can afford a servant to maintain the home that is his castle.

Free, privatized labor by women also benefits the superstructure of patriarchal society as a whole. In a cash economy where worth is determined by annual earnings, unpaid household work has no value, and by extension neither do the women who do it.[18] This philosophy allows women's work to be devalued even when it *is* taken into the paid labor market; "traditional" female jobs as teachers, nurses and secretaries, all of which have strong caretaking components, are among the lowest paid in our society. We pay the teachers of the next generation less than we pay telephone installers, for instance.[19] By refusing to acknowledge women's household contributions in calculations of the gross national product and those of the tax collector, society also avoids the cost of providing pensions, insurance and disability coverage.[20] By excluding unpaid female household labor, men have a larger financial pie to divvy up. (Although this is a rather simplified model of how our economic system allocates wealth, and ultimately other privileges, it is nonetheless accurate.)

As long as household technologies de-skill and devalue those who use them, as long as men are allowed to use "labor-saving" technology as an excuse not to share domestic labor, technology in the home cannot liberate the women who work there. Only when household services—like cooking, childcare, cleaning and others—are purchased in the marketplace, with a price tag prominently affixed, is the real value of women's contribution to the household acknowledged: for a woman with two young children, that contribution is, in the US, roughly $40,000 per year.[21]

[4]

Reach out and touch someone

The changes now underway in communications technology are nothing short of revolutionary: computer telecommunications, satellite teleconferencing, direct satellite-to-home broadcasting, cellular radio for mobile phones, high-capacity fiberoptic cables, interactive videotex services (text and graphic information delivered to a television screen or computer terminal via cable television or telephone line). But we need to think carefully about the consequences of these technologies, particularly for women, who are held responsible for relationships and human interconnection across time and distance. Communications technologies alter the ways in which we interact with others; in the past they have changed the frequency of contact (monthly by Pony Express, daily by telephone, hourly by radio news, constantly by video surveillance camera) and its nature (one-way radio broadcasts, two-way telephone calls).

Technology has expanded the forms of human communication from the original limitations of face-to-face conversation to include communications over distance by telegraph, telephone, television or satellite, and communications over time by written alphabet, printing press, audio recording, film or video cassette. Various technologies support interaction not only between two single points, as do telephones or letters, but from one-point-to-many-points simultaneously, as do newspapers or broadcasting, from many-points-to-one-point, as do satellite feeds to a television station, and even from many-points-to-many-others, as do CB radios or computer teleconferences.

New technology, old values

It is convenient, but inaccurate, to think that communications technology is transparent, that its only effect is to make it easier to contact someone else. Actually, technology defines our communication as much as transmits it. By changing the speed with which information travels and how far it can go, technology has even changed the *content* of what we communicate. There wasn't much point in an eighteenth-century woman sending a letter from Massachusetts to Virginia to discuss what to wear to a dance that night (or even in two weeks), but a lot of teenagers now spend Friday afternoons phoning each other about that crucial decision. Nor did it make sense to report up-to-the-minute traffic conditions on local roadways until radio came along. Technology can cause the loss of information, too. Illuminated manuscripts, for example, became exceedingly rare after the printing press was invented; the rich lore of oral cultures is inevitably thinned and compressed when recorded by film or television cameras.

New computer telecommunications services promise to have as phenomenal an impact on our lives and our children's as the telephone and television had on the last two generations. These simultaneous, multi-point to multi-point, two-way communication systems will offer mixed blessings before the end of this century. By hooking up modem-equipped computers to networks like The Source or CompuServe, users can already "chat" randomly via keyboard to everyone else on the network without calling them individually or even knowing who they are. (This is called an "unswitched" network, in contrast to dialing a specific telephone number from another phone on a "switched" network.)

In Britain, the Prestel system already delivers videotex displays of airline schedules, stock market figures, theater and sporting events, and descriptions of local restaurants. In France, the *électronique* experiment in Rennes provides the equivalent of an electronic telephone book, complete with Yellow Page advertisements. Telidon, the Canadian videotex experiment, offers similar services, while Viewtron, the first commercially offered American videotex service, is used for home banking and shopping. After scanning information on their home computers or special computer terminals, con-

LAST NIGHT, COMPUSERVE TURNED THIS COMPUTER INTO A TRAVEL AGENT FOR JENNIE, A STOCK ANALYST FOR RALPH, AND NOW, IT'S SENDING HERBIE TO ANOTHER GALAXY.

NO MATTER WHICH COMPUTER YOU OWN, WE'LL HELP YOU GET THE MOST OUT OF IT.

If you've got places to go, CompuServe can save you time and money getting there. Just access the Official Airline Guide Electronic Edition—for current flight schedules and fares. Make reservations through our on-line travel service. Even charter a yacht through "Worldwide Exchange."

If your money's in the market, CompuServe offers a wealth of prestigious financial data bases. Access Value Line, or Standard and Poor's. Get the latest information on 40,000 stocks, bonds or commodities. Then, consult experts like IDS or Heinold Commodities. All on line with CompuServe.

Or if, like Herbie, intergalactic gamesmanship is your thing, enjoy the best in fantasy, adventure, and space games. Like MegaWars, the ultimate computer conflict.

To get all this and more, you'll need a computer, a modem and CompuServe. CompuServe connects with almost any personal computer, terminal, or communicating word processor. To receive an illustrated guide to CompuServe and learn how you can subscribe, contact or call:

CompuServe
Consumer Information Service
2180 Wilson Road, Columbus, Ohio 43228
800-848-8199
In Ohio, call 614-457-8650

An H&R Block Company

Figure 4.1 CompuServe (*CompuServe Inc., Consumer Information Service*)

sumers can use these two-way systems to order tickets, purchase goods or make reservations. Once again technology is transferring activities that used to take place in public spaces back into the privacy of the home.

Changing our sense of space

To truly understand the particular impact these technologies will have on women's lives we need to consider what else women do, besides work, in public space, which the Greeks called the *agora* or marketplace. First and foremost, women are consumers. Keynesian economist John Kenneth Galbraith even suggested that women were kept out of the labor market in the 1950s and 1960s so that the unpaid work of consumption, more critical for the expansion of the postwar capitalist economy than for the maintenance of the household, could get done.[1]

Women are responsible for buying groceries, household products and clothing, but men generally participate in purchasing only the few "big ticket" items selected infrequently for each household, such as automobiles and financial services; men's only frequent purchases are liquor and beer.[2] Although women's expanding role in the labor force has changed buying decisions (women in America are now involved in choosing more than 50 percent of all automobiles and consumer electronics products, for instance[3]), most advertisers continue to play to old assumptions, placing computer ads in newspaper sports and business sections, which have higher male readership. Women, however, are still expected to stop at the market each evening to buy fresh vegetables, to run out for eggs, and to get the kids' dancing shoes. They are the ones who get the baby's prescription, remember a birthday card for their mother-in-law, and pick up coffee in the morning. Many men merely kick a tire or two every five years.

Second, women use public space to participate in important forms of social exchange. They may shop with friends, meet neighbors waiting in the check-out line, chat with strangers at the bus stop. If they lack the time to read the newspaper or

"I sincerely hope they don't develop shopping at home by computer until I unload all these coupons."

Figure 4.2 Computer shopping

watch TV, they can get news of the day, especially the unexpected sort, from conversations, flyers, headlines, ads in store windows and posters. In short, they can stay in touch with the "real" world on a superficial level by shopping, having their hair done, stopping at the bank, and picking up the kids at school. Especially for women who do not work outside the home, conversations with friends offer the critical stimulation and reinforcement necessary to keep from going crazy. (For men and women in the paid labor force, the workplace is the primary site of social exchange.)

When combined with the isolation of telecommuting, living better vicariously through videotex and home computers will drastically reduce women's reasons for leaving the house. This is no idle threat. Already the British, who have more computers and video recorders per capita than any other country, are spending more time in their homes and less at pubs, sporting events and the cinema.[4] Since shopping was previously considered "women's work," and since it will now be accomplished within the private (female) sphere, its New Age computer embodiment is not likely to move shopping suddenly into the column of men's household tasks.

In fact, home information services, like garbage disposals and dishwashers, may only increase the amount of time women spend on household chores. Videotex will make it "easier" for women to compare prices on "big ticket" items and increase the hours spent scanning video catalogs; more women may find themselves programming heating and air conditioning systems to conserve energy. By adding new items to the list of what a woman has to do, these systems will effectively swallow up any time she saves. Even for working mothers, for whom running fewer errands might closely approximate nirvana, real benefits may prove elusive. Poor Alice, running faster and faster to stay in the same place. . . .

Nor will these services be cheap. Although the French plan to offer everyone a free terminal, commercial services expect to charge, and charge big. As of 1983, US banks offering computerized home transactions were charging customers an average of $8-$12 per month for the privilege of having electronically paid bills debited immediately from their accounts. Knight-Ridder Newspapers, which offered the Viewtron service, expected its customers to pay $600 for their Sceptre terminals, plus a basic fee of $12 a month and an additional $1 an hour to the phone company; no wonder it has gone out of business! CompuServe, a computer network, charged $40 for a starter kit plus $6 an hour in the evenings and $12.50 an hour for daytime connection. In some cases users must also pay local and/or long-distance charges while they are hooked up; if they tie up their line with videotex services, they may need to install a second telephone line to receive regular phone calls.

In the worst case scenario, a class of information have-nots, unable to afford videotex information utilities, will be cut off from necessary information, especially if "old-fashioned" sources of information, such as libraries and customer service windows, disappear. And once again, as long as women's wages are lower than men's, women will reside disproportionately in the have-not class.

Picket-fenced, rose-covered, electronic cottages will change the nature of whom we talk to, as well as what we say. Instead of knowing the people around the block, we will know people around the world. Our "community" will not be based on who shares the same water main, school district, sewer line or political representative, but on who shares our interests, wherever they happen to live. Unfortunately, when we need someone to watch our children for a moment, to follow us to the garage when the car has to be repaired, or to lend a cup of sugar or some milk, a computer community just won't do. While we may gain strength of purpose from issue-oriented groups, voting is a matter of residence; unless we change political districts to correspond to membership in particular computer "SIGs" (special interest groups), we will lose far more political power than we gain by atomizing local neighborhoods into data-secure computer cottages. The arrogance of assuming that we can cut ourselves off from geographical proximity in favor of computer-mediated meetings of the minds is but another manifestation of the myth of self-sufficiency.

Articles in women's magazines (*Ms.*[5]) and general publications (*Village Voice*[6]) report women's fascination with computer communications, particularly "chatting" informally on modem-linked networks. Although this is partly a conditioned female response to the asocial, one-man, one-machine model of computer interaction, it also reflects problems with our *agora*s that computers only purport to solve. Like CB radio users, computer "chatters" select a nickname or "handle" that offers the protection of anonymity; but unlike CB, where gender is fairly easy to determine by voice, "chatting" provides total cover. Gender, race, sexual preference, environment, handicap and physical appearance are all irrelevant. For perhaps the first and only time in their lives, women's comments are judged without reference to their legs. No whistles, no catcalls, no fears of rape, mugging or assault—computer "chatting" offers women the freedom to walk, talk, socialize and fantasize without becoming a victim of misogynistic culture.

Maybe we should be grateful for a technology that makes at least this opportunity available, even though we ought to be able to experience such freedom without being electronically disembodied. But while applauding women who use computers to meet this very human need, we must resist the temptation to see this technology as a solution to the problems that exist in the physical environment. We need to acknowledge that agoraphobia, a fear of open, public space that predominantly affects married women, results not from a personal phobia but from an *agora* that doesn't function for half the population.[7] We cannot afford the complacency that suggests computerized communication is an adequate solution to the overwhelming presence of street harassment, sexually exploitative advertising, pornographic violence and rape that makes each and every woman vulnerable each and every time she walks out her door.

Changing our sense of time

In a peculiarly Einsteinian twist, it is space—street space, urban planning, travel distance—that warps our sense of time. We cannot, therefore, consider communications technology apart from the transportation, architectural and urban planning technologies that determine how long it takes to move around the space we live in. We nonchalantly describe the distance between two places as a "40-minute drive," remind ourselves that "it will take an entire afternoon to get there and back by bus," warn guests to "leave an hour early because of the traffic," and tell tourists "you can't get there from here." A woman's ability to accomplish her gender-linked daily tasks, from going to work to picking up the kids at school, from doing the shopping to stopping at the laundromat, depends on being able to get from one place to another. Perhaps if our cities were better planned or our public transit systems better organized, we would not need to let our fingers do the walking on computer keyboards; our feet could do it quite well.

Part of the problem rests with post-World War II suburban housing developments and part with the ubiquitous presence of the automobile. The confluence of these two technologies has resulted in workplaces remote from home sites, distances to neighborhood services easy to drive, but too great to walk,

Figure 4.3 Getting around the city becomes more difficult every day (*Connecticut Department of Transportation*)

population density too thin for cost-effective mass transit, roads following scenic, not short, routes, and many postwar housewives isolated in gilded, suburban cages.

These consequences arose not from mere circumstance, but from deliberate efforts to replace efficient, non-polluting trolley and electric car systems with diesel buses, and later automobiles. Between 1936 and 1955, the United States lost 35,000 of its 40,000 streetcars to motorized buses, in spite of the fact that trolley systems effectively met local traffic needs. General Motors, Firestone Tire and Standard Oil of California colluded in the purchase and destruction of the intercity rail company and electric streetcar companies in Los Angeles, for instance. In city after city, these companies "purchased the local system, scrapped its electric transit cars, tore down its power transmission lines, ripped up the tracks, and placed

49

General Motors diesel buses fueled by Standard Oil on . . . crowded streets.[8]

To further complicate the situation, zoning ordinance in the US frequently mandate large lot sizes, reduce housing density per acre, and forbid the mixed commercial and residential use of an area or a building.[9] Consequently, women must now calculate the best path to save time and gas, they must chauffeur children and elderly relatives who can't drive to meetings, parties and doctor's appointments, and they must somehow combine the challenge of working both inside and outside the home.

This challenge is further aggravated by inadequate, deteriorating, ever-more-costly transit services. Public transit is designed to get men from home to work and back again; after all, they designed it to meet *their* needs. It does not function well for a working mother who has to stop by the day care center, dry cleaner and butcher shop on her way home; it does not provide transportation at hours or to places needed by children and the elderly. Studies in the US show that women comprise approximately two-thirds of all public transport users, yet buses and trains do not meet their needs for multiple short trips.[10] Only high-density, center cities, like New York City and London, with extensive mass transit systems, escape this pattern. Owning a car is often essential for a woman's survival, but a 1978 US study shows that when a two-worker family owns only one car, it is the man who drives it more often.[11]

There are both social and technological means of solving the transport problem, but the collective will to do so is lacking. From a technological perspective, computers could be used to route and schedule demand-based, mini-jitney services, offering door-to-door transport service within residential districts to children, the elderly and adults without cars. The cost seems high compared to offering limited work-to-home bus routes only because women's unpaid labor running errands and playing chauffeur is never included in any of the cost/benefit equations. Once again, if market services replaced privatized ones, the true value of uncompensated female labor would be obvious.

Social changes, such as the introduction of flexible hours

and job-sharing, will only somewhat simplify women's travel lives, since women usually preselect a job that will correspond to their complicated schedules. Since such alternatives have been implemented to save energy, reduce pollution and eliminate traffic congestion, it is worth trying to deliberately restructure them to serve women's needs as well. Most important, from a social perspective, women's gender-defined status in both the home and the workplace must be changed so that they have equal resources with which to purchase travel alternatives and so that chores are more equitably distributed among household members. Only when those changes are achieved, according to transport sociologist Genevieve Giuliano, will "the uniqueness of women's travel needs . . . disappear; [will] women's travel needs . . . become people's travel needs, and [will] transportation policy . . . be developed on that basis."[12]

With enough public demand, legislators could alter zoning regulations, require banks to finance mixed-used buildings, support the construction of light-rail systems, re-design master plans to encourage high-density housing, "in-filling," or renovation of existing neighborhoods, and insist that developers integrate convenient shopping and childcare services and provide local transit alternatives in new developments. The role of human hands and corporate profits in implementing technology is most apparent, perhaps, in the shape of our cities and the ways we struggle through them.

High-tech, high-touch?

The "high-tech, high-touch" phenomenon that John Naisbitt describes in his book *Megatrends*[13] is another symptom of technological development gone awry. According to his theory, the more that technology assumes cold, hard-surfaced, alienating forms, the more people seek warmth, texture, and the comfort of human contact to counteract it. The question, of course, is why does new technology diminish the relationship between craftsworkers and their tools; why does it isolate people from one another? Why do skyscrapers look like glass eggcrates instead of towering redwoods? Why are computers

51

made of plastic instead of wood, fur, or "terrycloth," as Alvin Toffler suggests? Why are robots articulated metal instead of animated mannequins? Why are we talking to each other through video screens? Why do our contemporary artifacts look and function the way they do and who designs them anyway?

Most engineers would answer impatiently that the appearance of tools is determined by their intended application, cost of production, appropriateness of structure to purpose, ease of manufacture, and suitability of materials to form and function. Except for the last response (permanent homes cannot be construted from papier-mâché; fur or fabric that holds static charge cannot be used for electronic components; cake frosting cannot be used for a desk top), these answers merely beg the real question, which is one of value.

Value is set by a complex and continuously changing interplay among such factors as the relative scarcity of resources (gold has a greater value than water), the demand for them (if you are lost in the desert, water is more valuable than gold), and, most important, hidden assumptions about what matters. (Commented the man who paid $10,000 to buy a state-of-the-art Swiss bobsled for the losing American team at the 1984 Winter Olympics, "Price/value relationship has no place here.") While scarcity and demand play a role in selecting among the alternative ways of executing a conceived design, it is hidden assumptions about what something "should" look like that drive an "idea" into its tangible form: one form appears intrinsically more valuable than others.

On some Platonic and probably subconscious level, every engineer, architect, planner or inventor has an "end" in mind when she or he starts working; the very definition of technology, as opposed to basic research or artistic endeavor, is to produce a tool or method to achieve a practical end. To this end, he (in this culture most of them *are* "he"s) attaches certain qualities to the physical embodiment of his idea. Both the idea and its associated qualities, whether they arise from the traditional "light bulb" or are assigned by the company marketing department, carry an invisible load of moral, ethical, religious, spiritual, emotional, rational, psychological, social and technological assumptions. Those assumptions shadow the idea all the way through its design, execution, marketing, purchase and use, in spite of extensive market research or the push/pull of consumer demand. And there, as they say, is the rub.

Only certain members of our society are either chosen or self-select to become members of the elite community of engineers, architects, planners, and inventors who shape the "man-made" world; they don't necessarily share the values or assumptions of the people who have to live in the world they create. Those who choose to work with "things" frequently identify themselves as unhappy working with people; they are loners, uncomfortable with "messy" emotions, who can relax with a predictable machine but fear an unpredictable human soul.[14] They are also overwhelmingly male.[15] While there is a gender gulf of biology, experience, expectation and socialization between the sexes in our society, no men are on a farther shore than engineers.[16]

Our communications technologies are invented by men who don't like to talk to other people.[17] Our offices are designed by men who prefer isolation. Our cities are laid out by men who crave distance from others. Our utilities are generated by men who prefer to depend on machines than on other human beings. We have eggcrate skyscrapers as phallic monuments, cold surfaces devoid of dread emotion, hard-edged forms that suppress feeling, alienating technology built by lonely, alienated men who want a protective shield from the noisy rat-a-tat-tat of life.

We seek high-touch refuge from high-tech because the human being has been left out; the female part of all of us is missing and we miss it. If that doesn't explain why we need many more women engineers, nothing will.

[5]

Don't bother your pretty little head

Except when women in tribal cultures managed to assert for themselves a recognized role in production and subsistence and hence were allowed to pray for rain and fertility, men took for themselves the responsibility and honor of tribal relationships with the deity. Sacred dances, from the spear dance by the Wogogo tribesmen of East Africa to the snake dance of the Hopi Indians, sacred music, from the trumpets forbidden to Pygmy women to Gregorian chants, and religious art, from the animal masks of New Guinea tribes to the cathedral of Notre Dame—all were part of the male realm. In the modern world, where science and technology have displaced the gods of rain and wisdom, men still constitute most of the high priests worshipping at the laboratory altar. With the exhilarating exception of Sally Ride and a few other women astronauts, outer space still belongs to a male club with the "right stuff." Our exotic weapons of destruction—neutron bombs, blinding laser beams, killer satellites—are completely under male control. Condescendingly, men tell women "not to bother your pretty little head" with such worrisome "big" technologies, or with many other worrisome little ones.

In the process of dividing labor according to gender, both inside the house and outside, we have also divided ideas, concepts, concerns and issues into "soft" subjects that women "ought" to deal with and "hard" ones they shouldn't. Women are expected to care about vacuum cleaners, welfare programs and the school play, while men are expected to care about bulldozers, stock market prices and arms control. Obviously, the concept of gender-based division of labor is not unique to technological development, but we often ignore the fact that this concept informs new technologies just as much as it has old ones. We can see its dangerous tracks on both the work we do with our hands and the work we do with our head.

Dividing the world: hands

Robots for factory automation . . . computers for office automation . . . techniques for manufacturing silicon chips and solar cells . . . gene splicing . . . nuclear power plants. New jobs in new technologies, all right, but not for women. By 1979 these fields had opened up more than three million jobs in the United States,[1] but women hold very few of them, especially at the technical level. (Depending on the field, women's participation ranges roughly from 5-25 percent of all engineers, scientists and technicians.[2]) As in more traditional job categories, women's jobs are concentrated at the lower end of the pay scale. Whether a woman assembles circuit boards or plucks chickens, she still makes only about $4.50 or £3 an hour, and she still makes less than men doing the same job.[3]

Neither women's increased participation in the labor force nor the loss of high-paying, unionized, male jobs in the old industrial fields of coal mining, steel production and car manufacture has appreciably narrowed the wage gap; US women earned 64 cents to the male dollar in 1955, 59 cents in 1981, and 62 cents in 1982. In the UK women have not fared much better. In 1983, women working full-time earned 64.5 percent of what men were paid.[4] On a broad social level, this situation will not improve in the short term. Although high-technology industries forecast phenomenal growth over the next ten years, the expansion of low-paying, predominantly female, service jobs will be more than five times the projected growth in high-technology employment.[5] Unless the concept of equal pay for work of comparable worth becomes a reality, new technology will not erase the boundary between women's work and men's work, but rather will redraw it in indelible ink.

For instance, three-quarters of women's jobs in the

computer field are in the low-paying categories of keypunch, data entry and computer operations, while three-quarters of men's jobs are in the much more remunerative fields of machine repair, programming, systems analysis and other computer specialties. Female computer professionals in the US earn only 75 percent of men's wages; the average wage disparity over all computer occupations is $5000 to $7000 each year—enough for a small car, a year's rent, or an annual college tuition bill.[6] Only one percent of female computer professionals earn more than $50,000 a year, which is generally considered the dividing line between middle management and the executive suite.

Although Ada Byron Lovelace programmed the world's first computer (Charles Babbage's differential engine) in 1840 and women like Captain Grace Hopper (US Naval Reserves) programmed the Mark I, one of the first modern computers, during and after World War II, their contributions were considered exceptional. At first, programming was considered a routine, clerical task (female), but later, as computer technology matured, programming was elevated to an esoteric realm for "wizards" (male). Partly because there were few formal opportunities to learn computer science in schools (learning took place on an *ad hoc* basis in science and engineering centers where computers were plentiful and women were scarce), women's participation was set back nearly twenty years. When colleges started to offer training in computer science in the late 1960s, women began to enter the field in greater numbers. Now that women constitute nearly 30 percent of all programmers, programming is once again becoming a routine, clerical job through the use of automatic program generators, structured programming techniques and packaged applications software.[7] A July 1980 issue of *Computerworld* unintentionally headlined the irony. One story read, "Programmers seen needing fewer skills," while another in the same issue announced, "Project opens computer science jobs to women."[8]

Computing is not alone, of course. Even the young, nontraditional practitioners of appropriate technologies in the Aquarian Age can't avoid pervasive job segregation. Anecdotal evidence shows women in charge of gardening, food preservation, aquaculture and worm farming, men in charge of alternative energy sources—solar, wind, hydro and biomass.[9] The biological sciences have always been friendlier to women than the physical sciences, but even here there is segregation. Genetic engineering and molecular biology sport tweedy "masculine" labels, whereas physiology and botany flirt with "feminine" tags. (This fact makes 1983 Nobel Laureate Barbara McClintock's achievement in elucidating the role of "jumping genes" of Indian corn all the more spectacular; her recognition was thirty years late.)

Partially as a consequence of discriminatory employment in many fields, new technology encourages its own discriminatory application. The ubiquitous computer enables management to record keystroke and error rates for typists and data entry personnel, to pay piecework rates for information processing, and to implement work speed-ups. In 1981 The National Institute for Occupational Safety and Health found that clerical workers using video display terminals (VDTs) exhibit higher levels of job stress than any other category of workers ever studied, including air traffic controllers. By comparison, professional writers and editors using VDTs, who control the pace of their own work and receive recognition for it, have the lowest stress.[10] Women, of course, hold 95 percent of those high-stress clerical VDT job slots.[11]

Similarly, women suffer disproportionately from the work rationalization or de-skilling effects of most office automation schemes. Rationalization is the division of labor into ever finer, more specialized tasks. In many automated offices secretarial work is now divided so that one person does word processing all day, another does electronic filing, and a third answers the phone.[12] Women who have recently entered middle management are equally vulnerable. Writer Barbara Garson quotes an executive who describes the future corporate structure quite graphically:[13]

> We are moving from the pyramid shape to the Mae West. The employment chart of the future will still show those swellings on the top, and we'll never completely get rid of those big bulges of clerks on the bottom. What we're trying to do right now is pull in that waistline (expensive middle management and skilled secretaries).

57

"And this model will do the work of eighteen men . . . or five women."

Figure 5.1 In spite of their greater productivity, women will still be the ones displaced by office automation (Machine Design, *Leonard Todd, cartoonist*)

Computers and other new forms of office technology—electronic mail, tele-facsimile, voice store-and-forward message systems, voice and optical character recognizers—offer management new opportunities to control a female work-force that has just started to organize; the technology itself does not demand that those opportunities be seized. A sensitive company could implement office automation in humanitarian ways to increase productivity and reduce error rates, but still offer job diversification, create career ladders and save jobs. In reality, though, the men at the top who control the process are increasingly distant from the women controlled by it.

Other technologies find different razors to slice labor into similar gender divisions. In the case of hazardous new manufacturing processes, for example, women of childbearing age may be excluded from employment unless they agree to be sterilized. In 1978 five women needed their jobs at American Cyanamid's Willow Bend, West Virginia, pigment plant so badly that they underwent sterilization rather than be demoted to lower-paying jobs.[14] Focusing on women's unsuitability as a class, whether or not they intend to have children, diverts attention from the fact that jobs hazardous to women's reproductive systems may be just as hazardous to men's; efforts should be directed to make the jobs safe for both.

Genetic screening offers another means of excluding women from the workplace. Seventeen companies in the United States have already begun using this technique (and forty-two more intend to), ostensibly to identify workers who may be susceptible to occupational diseases caused by environmental pollutants. This rather inaccurate screening method can be used to discriminate against women with "faulty genes."[15]

Robotics, which is seen as a threat to "male" jobs on assembly lines in heavy industry, is concurrently identified as a new career opportunity for displaced male workers. Robotics will also displace the predominantly female workers who assemble electronics, manufacture textiles, inspect and test products, or pack and wrap goods,[16] but no one talks about retraining women to produce or supervise their robotic replacements. In a typical Catch-22, women are offered no training opportunities, yet they are excluded from this new field because they lack appropriate skills.

The new automation: who puts the coffee in the coffee pot?

"I thought we spent all that money on the machine because they said the operators never had to sit around and do nothing." Typist Ellen Levy still shudders when she thinks of that remark, made by her boss's wife while Ellen waited for the computer to finish printing out a job.[17] The temptation is so great to identify the worker with her equipment that the person behind the work disappears in a fog of words: "When can your machine do this?" Human beings become the machines they operate: word processors, keypunchers, spinners, stampers. The identification becomes so pervasive that supervisors wonder, "If the machine is doing all the work, why is it taking so long?"

When computers, electric weed clippers, robots, microwave ovens and digitally controlled coffeemakers are taken for granted, the labor involved becomes invisible. But someone still has to run the weed clipper, prepare the meal, enter data, put coffee in the coffeemaker and throw away the old grounds. Particularly when that someone is a woman, whose labor is likely to be either unpaid or underpaid, we forget that work is even required. Such invisibility is particularly destructive to women since new technologies disperse the work done by paid female labor to unpaid female consumers.

Banking or paying bills by computer, touch-tone phone, or videotex, for instance, will result in extensive job loss for bank tellers, bookkeepers, record-keepers and clerical workers, all female jobs. We know that the work these women do is valuable; Citibank in New York charges customers who have less than $500 in their accounts 25 cents for every transaction with a human being, instead of with an automatic teller machine (ATM). (The bank tried to limit "live" teller services to customers whose minimum balance was $5,000, but public outrage forced them to devise a less offensive, but equally income-discriminatory, formula. Can you imagine waiting outside on a cold, rainy day to use an ATM?[18])

Companies whose accounts will be electronically credited when clients "dial-their-dollars-direct" from home will collectively save millions of dollars that they now spend on clerical and bookkeeping services. They ought to *pay* their customers for the savings they will realize, but of course they won't. Hey, we're suppose to be grateful for the convenience; after all, we're not standing in the rain waiting in line, are we?

When people start checking out their food, shoes and jogging suits on home TV screens, retail clerks and grocery checkers will join the unemployment line, right behind the tellers and billing clerks. Hard-working librarians will be next, since videotex will offer a handy substitute for the library services cut during an era of tight budgets. And don't forget the airplane reservation clerks and ticket sellers, whose jobs will also fall prey to the green screen. The telephone company already has replaced live voices and real people with speech synthesizers that provide forwarding numbers, time, weather and directory assistance.

Unpaid consumers, primarily women, will be doing the work women used to be paid to do. In 1982 females in the US made up 60 percent of all retail sales clerks, 85 percent each of librarians, billing clerks and cashiers, 92 percent of telephone operators, 94 percent of bank tellers, and 98 percent of telephone receptionists—all occupations that will become obsolete in the Information Age. On the other half of the great gender divide, men will come out ahead with new technology. In 1982 in the US they held the overwhelming percentage of jobs for which demand will rise as home information services proliferate: 78 percent of all shipping clerks; 90 percent of electronic technicians; 94 percent of delivery services and route workers, 95 percent each of TV, computer, and home appliance repair and installation technicians.[19] Look at it this way: all those unpaid female consumers will have been really well trained!

Dividing the world: head

Compared to its obvious effects on what we do, computer technology has far more subtle effects on what we think, what we know, and what we think we know. The computer, through databases, printouts, and the machine itself, has begun to alter the way we arrange, classify and evaluate information, such as the alphabet rearranged the way our ancestors understood sounds. Since most "computer people" don't care about these effects, and most computer novices are still struggling to reconstruct a lost file, the most significant implications of the information revolution escape notice. Unless we become aware of these implications, the slippery floor of reality may slide right out from under us.

First of all, people treat printed and numerical information from a computer as more valid and more important than information from a filing cabinet, a book, or someone's head. Thirteen-inch wide, green-barred paper with holes along the edges and a dot-matrix typeface does not guarantee that what's printed on it is any good. Yet people apparently suspend their sense of judgment and assume that just because information comes from a computer, it must be accurate, current and complete. It's often not. The abuses by airline companies that provide computerized ticket reservation databases to travel agents were so flagrant, for example, that the Civil Aeronautics Board had to forbid preferential listings with a built-in bias toward the owners' routes.[20]

We do not have the computer equivalent of a critical research tradition to decide if a signature is forged, a manuscript old, or a source worthy; worse yet, we don't realize what we don't know; we aren't teaching people to treat computer output with a little healthy skepticism. In 1982 *Psychology Today* magazine reported an experiment with a calculator programmed to give wrong answers to straight-forward arithmetic problems (e.g. $252 \times 1.2 = 452$). Only 20 percent of the subjects realized the calculator was wrong after the first exercise, even if the calculator was off by as much as 50 percent.[21]

Second, since the computer has made it easier to collect data, we have acquired overwhelming amounts of it, without considering whether or not it is important or useful to have. As a result, we are swimming in redundancy and sinking in "facts." Already, it seems impossible to sort out which information is essential for survival in an overly complex world, and the computer revolution has barely begun.

Third, the keyword structure for searching databases makes it difficult to skim a databank for random information the way the eye scans newspaper headlines for an interesting article. Sometimes it is important to learn the unexpected and discover the unsought. Suppose, for instance, we program a videotex-supplied, electronic newspaper to produce all stories in the category of "local news" and all articles containing the keywords "baseball scores" and "nuclear weapons." How will we find out if a UFO has landed, if the United States has invaded Grenada again, or if Jane Fonda gave a speech fifty miles away? Contrary to Pasteur's famous dictum, chance favors the open mind, not the prepared one.

"Keyword comprehension" like this poses a special hazard for women, whose lives have been left out of history books, psychological theories, biological experiments, and language itself. *No* computerized database exists for women's studies because the major, commercially supported databases, such as Lockheed's DIALOG or System Development Corporation's ORBIT, do not consider it financially rewarding.[22] Women may exist; it just isn't profitable to let anyone know. As a result, searching for information about "women and . . ." becomes an expensive exercise in frustration. When Jaime Horwitz, an environmental psychologist in New York, decided to search the ERIC (Educational Resources and Information Center) database in 1976 for articles containing the keywords "women" and "environment," the computer produced one reference: an article attributing the extinction of numerous animals to the vanity of women and their desire for fur on their backs. If it weren't so tragic, it might by funny.

But women, who have been ignored, neglected, and omitted, can't afford to be deleted, too, so the National Council for Research on Women, together with the American Library Association and the Business and Professional Women's Foundation, plans to establish a comprehensive, computerized database that would incorporate the massive amounts of unindexed information located in women's centers around the country. Their Data Base Project will also establish categories and descriptors to shape common files and improve access to the new database via a software translator.[23]

In the UK, WATCH, a database on women and technical change, has been created by Christine Zmroczek and Felicity Henwood at the Science Policy Research Unit (SPRU) at the University of Sussex. WATCH cannot yet be accessed by computer modem, but searches can be made by SPRU staff. In addition, the catalog of the Feminist Library in London is also being computerized. At last, a database of one's own!

Very few people realize that most databases are privately owned, profit-making ventures. Expensive (anywhere from $30 to $300 per hour, plus 10 to 20 cents per listing), privatized information banks like these put limits on access as well as content; unlike the public library, databases allow you to buy only the information you can afford. The "free" market alone controls who enters data, who decides what goes in and what gets left out, what degree of accuracy is cost-effective, and how much security is reasonable. No organization certifies databases for quality or requires that they include all published material; databases operate on their own recognizance, under the illusion of objectivity and the cover of the computer. Freedom of the press used to belong to anyone who could afford a press; soon it will belong only to those who can afford to create and maintain a database.

The incremental changes wrought by computerized information systems may seem to be too minute to worry about now, but they will ultimately, and irrevocably, change our way of knowing the world. The more that errors and omissions about women, Blacks, Hispanics and Asians become ingrained, repeated, compounded, amplified and accepted through a database, the more difficult it will be to construct an alternative world view. It will be increasingly hard to distinguish fiction from fact, myth from reality, fairy tale from history. People may recognize that books have biases, errors and omissions, but they rarely recognize that computers do. The real meaning of computer literacy, then, may not be in learning how to plug it in and turn it on, but in knowing when to turn it off.

[6]

The bad math of zero sum technology

According to many capitalist economists and politicians, resources and power are allocated according to Calvinistic-sounding principles; everyone gets what they deserve, whether God, the free market, or Santa Claus handles the distribution. If our portion isn't big enough when the finite pie—be it money, oil, jobs or mincemeat—is sliced up, then we are supposed to go home and pull ourselves up by the bootstraps so we'll deserve a bigger slice next year. The primary assumption behind this metaphor—that the pie stays the same size—implies that whenever someone gets a bigger piece, someone else has to get a smaller one: life is one great big zero sum.

In many cases, new technology can increase the size of the pie or put more goodies in it. To carry the analogy further, new technology may enlarge the pie by developing a cheaper way to maintain flavor in quantity (e.g. imitation vanilla extract), a mechanical harvester for grapes that reduces labor costs, or a new tool, such as an extra-long rolling pin. But people who believe that reality is a zero sum eat their small slices without realizing that, thanks to technology, someone else may now be swallowing a second slice of a larger pie.

Technology is used as a vehicle not only to enlarge the pie, but also to decide who will get to eat it. Although technological development may dramatically increase both the gross sales and net profit of a product, an individual worker is often unaware of this. Rather, she or he judges new earnings against past earnings, not against her or his share of the larger pot of gold (the bigger pie) now available; those who provide capital (investors or stockholders), not labor, are the ones who divide up the increased profits. The textile manufacturing technologies developed during the Industrial Revolution clearly demonstrate how this inequitable distribution takes place.

Rose-colored glasses, rose-covered cottages

Cottage industry, or "putting out," first became popular during the early stages of the Industrial Revolution. Prior to that time, each household had manufactured fabric and clothing from start to finish, with all members of the household sharing both the work and the money made by selling surplus goods. Spinning wheels and looms had been owned by the family, which controlled the tempo and quality of its work; housework had been a visible part of the seamless web of tasks whose completion allowed the family to survive. But by the mid-eighteenth century, entrepreneurs who owned the new carding machines and water-powered spinning frames that had been developed to speed up textile manufacture took control of the production process.[1]

The entrepreneurs rationalized production by "putting out" the separate tasks of cleaning, spinning, drying, weaving and sewing to different households, which then competed to provide the greatest output at the lowest prices. Initially, the cash income of the cottage industry household rose, but at the cost of reduced activity in the barter economy.[2] As the Industrial Revolution continued, new inventions like water- and steam-powered looms provided the impetus to centralize production in factories. By 1790 the brief age of "putting out" was over. Centralized factories increased output, as expected, but they also further divided textile work into the specific, repetitive tasks done by speeders, drawers, dressers and warpers. In the process, workers lost money and entrepreneurs and investors made it.

Under the factory system, the family wage disappeared and the net purchasing power of the household decreased.[3] Employers paid low wages for relatively unskilled tasks, continually reduced piecework pay rates to keep earnings

Figure 6.1 Drawing in: shuttle loom (*Merrimack Valley Textile Museum*)

down, and at least one former cash-earner, often the wife, had to remain at home to provide childcare and support services for all the family members employed outside the home.[4] (Even at that time, single women working in the mills earned, on the average, only 57 cents for every male dollar. The lowest factory wage for men was almost invariably greater than the highest wage for women.)[5]

On the other hand, the investors who put up capital to buy equipment earned enormous profits. For one textile firm, the Boston Manufacturing Company, sales skyrocketed from $3000 annually in 1814 to more than 100 times that figure eight years later. Between 1814 and 1823 the company's assets grew almost twentyfold, increasing from $39,000 to $771,000.[6] The company paid its investors 20 percent dividends every year between 1817 and 1825, but laborers' wages—and household income—did not keep pace.[7] Textile technology spread its impact throughout the entire society, but its rewards were distributed more narrowly.

Although the cottage industry mentality compared rather favorably to factory-based, mass-production techniques, it still separated housework from "productive" labor. In many cases, housework that had been shared by all members of the artisan family devolved solely upon women, while other family members concentrated on producing goods that brought in cash. Since cash payment was associated with textile labor inside the home, but not with the effort women expended on housework, cottage industries contributed to the devaluation of women's work. The much-acclaimed computerized retreat to the electronic cottage thus appears less a vision of "progress" than a backwards glance through a rear-view mirror. Rather than a stop *en route* to an even better artisan age, the electronic cottage heralds another form of owner-controlled, supervised and rationalized labor. Perhaps poet Paul Valery, who said that "the future is not what it used to be," had only the half of it; the past doesn't seem to be what it used to be, either.

The global assembly line

In the decentralized factory of the future, the worker will buy her/his own tools (i.e. a computer and peripherals) and absorb all overhead costs—rent, heat, equipment insurance, telephone connection charges and installation fees (if one line is continually tied up for computer transmission, the worker must install another line for calls), electrical usage, and installation of a power supply that is more stable than the one electrical utilities usually provide to residences. In addition, employees are likely to lose opportunities for promotion (promotion usually means becoming a supervisor, but there will be fewer workers to supervise), to receive lower earnings because of competitive, piecework payment or flat-rate, contract wage schemes, and to forfeit benefits (for example, will a company pay worker's compensation for an employee working at home? Will home workers become self-employed, independent subcontractors liable for all social security taxes, instead of half? Revisions in the 1983 US tax code cite these very consequences as a defintiion of the term "independent contractor").

If workers don't accept the wonderful ways in which new technology decreases employers' costs, they will be out of luck. Already, "offshore offices" are following runaway factories to the cheap labor of the Sunbelt and the Third World. George R. Simpson, chairman of Satellite Data Corporation, says his company relays printed materials by satellite from New York to Barbados, where data entry clerks are paid only $1.50 an hour. As he recently told *Business Week* magazine, "We can do the work in Barbados for less than it costs in New York to pay for floor space. . . . The economics are so compelling that a company could take a whole building in Hartford, Connecticut, and transfer the whole function to India or Pakistan."[8]

Already, similar economic arguments have been used to justify transferring electronics assembly jobs to the Export Processing Zones (EPZs) of developing countries. Eighty-five to 90 percent of the workers on the global assembly line are female; since most are single and under the age of 25, they are expected to submit docilely to patterns of domination within the factory that mimic traditional patriarchal family relationships.[9] For the manufacturer, the global assembly line offers great savings. Hourly wages that average $4.50 in the United States are typically reduced to hourly rates of $1.15 in Hong Kong, 90 cents in Mexico, 48 cents in Malaysia, or 19 cents in Indonesia.[10] Shipping costs on lightweight components are low, and the components are taxed only on the value added in the overseas assembly process (for example, soldering fine gold wires to the microscopic integrated circuits etched on a silicon chip). For large production runs, "packing" various chips onto a board is usually done overseas, but small runs are often "jobbed out" to minority women in industrial nations. The seemingly endless supply of cheap, female labor in Asia

69

Figure 6.2 Detailed work on the global assembly line (*Lynn Duggan, photographer*)

and Latin America obviates any need to provide decent benefits, good working conditions, protection for workers' health, promotional opportunities, or job enrichment; the resulting high job turnover rate is welcomed as a means of discouraging unionization.[11]

As long as the profits of new technology return primarily to those who finance it, rather than to those who produce it, international capital will continue to flow to Third World countries so those profits can be maximized. Manufacturers argue that cheap overseas labor is the only way to produce competitively priced goods, a red herring that distracts attention from the millions of dollars spent on advertising, marketing, packaging, promotion, executive salaries, bonuses, "golden parachutes" (benefits for executives who lose their jobs) and dividends. There are, in fact, many other ways to produce competitively priced goods; the question is: from whose pocket will the competitive edge be picked?

Pulling out the plums

There are other subtle ways in which women get the zero end of the technological stick. Government money spent on research and development, particularly in the defense sector, provides far more jobs to men than to women. Recent US studies show that women hold fewer than 30 percent of the 18,000 jobs created per billion dollars of defense spending—and that percentage goes mainly for secretarial and clerical workers.[12] Increasing demand for electrical and aviation engineers, metalworkers, and electronics technicians does not increase job opportunities for women, who have been systematically deterred from entering these fields. Furthermore, since civilian spending creates more jobs than defense spending, women lose an additional 9,500 jobs for every billion dollars spent on weaponry.[13]

Simultaneous budget cuts in social programs have resulted in disproportionate job loss by females, who do 70 percent of the nation's human services work.[14] One analysis showed that women held 45 percent of the government jobs lost to budget cuts in the US at the federal level between 1981 and 1983, although they accounted for only 33 percent of the federal workforce. Women administrators really felt the brunt of the shift from social to defense spending; they were laid off at a rate 150 percent higher than male administrators.[15]

Some women's organizations have tried to fight back. The Women's Technical Institute in Boston, established in 1981, grew out of a federally funded effort called Project ACT, which encouraged women to train for such nontraditional, high-tech occupations as drafting, computer repair, technical illustration and electronics.[16] Similar projects have been established in the UK, training women for nontraditional jobs including those related to new technologies. The oldest, the East Leeds Women's Workshop, was established in 1981, while the Haringey Women's Training and Education Centre started in 1983.

The danger in some of these job-training activities is that they are training women for jobs, like drafting, that will not be there when the women finish learning. Sociologist Sally L. Hacker has reported that women who were trained to occupy nontraditional skilled and semi-skilled crafts positions (e.g. telephone installation, framework, pole climbing) for the "old" American Telephone & Telegraph (AT&T) between 1972 and 1975 were deliberately encouraged to enter jobs intended for automation within five years. As a result of AT&T's "affirmative action" employment program, more men were hired for "women's jobs" than women were hired for "men's jobs."[17] Progress, in this case, had a strong backwards vector.

It is easy to "blame the victim" in these situations; to say that it's up to the individual woman to train for the expanding high-tech career opportunities of the 1980s and 1990s. But it is very difficult for women to overcome years of conditioning away from such occupations, to put up with hostility and harassment on the job, to overcome "stacked decks" in union apprenticeship programs, or to pay for training programs while they are working for low wages in traditional jobs. According to Mary Walshok's study in *Blue Collar Women*, women who have been able to withstand the rigors of working in such blue-collar occupations as airplane maintenance and plumbing have exceptional drive, very high levels of self-confidence, and a family background that includes independent experiences, strong mothers, and access to nontraditional occupational skills.[18]

But working women should not have to qualify as heroines to get a job in new technology. Further, it is clear that the number of high-tech jobs will not be as great as the hype that surrounds them, and that new technology merely sustains the traditional gender-division of labor. The unequal division of the big-pie-in-the-future-sky is not a technological problem that individuals can solve; it is a social problem that demands a collective, political solution.

The heated debate over national re-industrialization policies could be linked to a new form of affirmative action, but unless women raise their voices they are likely to see only a post-industrial equivalent of the postwar era, when women were forced to give up their jobs to men returning from war. The media recognizes that men displaced from their jobs in the steel and automobile industries are victims of the shift to an information economy, but women, who have suffered since the early stages of the Industrial Age, are invisible victims of the same shift. Currently, a narrow window of opportunity exists to provide job equity in the new age: training programs can be opened to both men and women, whether unemployed, never employed, underemployed, or displaced; comparable worth issues can be addressed as new occupations are created; men can shoulder an increasing share of household labor as the length of their paid work week declines; and "new" wealth can be redistributed through tax and income plans.

But without a sweeping, concrete plan to decentralize control over new technology, it will be impossible to avoid the "Third-Worldization" of the First World—a process that would exacerbate the gap between the rich and the poor, decimate the middle class, and create a large, lower class of desperate service workers. Existing power relationships set one group off against another in competition for a limited number of jobs in an economy interpreted as a zero sum.

As new technology is developed and marketed, it warps the complex, implicit barter system of labor and value that we maintain among ourselves and with the physical world. Since we don't, as a society, set explicit values for new technology— we don't decide what labor is worth which goods—those who control the technology are allowed to imply that the mysterious workings of the mythical free market have somehow set a price. And those prices determine how the technological pie gets divided, who profits and who suffers.

We know that the value of technology floats; just look at the $1000 price contractors charge the US Department of Defense for a simple, 26-cent, plastic cap; imagine how inflated the price of a computer may be! By divorcing ourselves from the process of technological change, we lose any notion of value and find ourselves in that disturbing, indeterminate world in which all forms of currency are floating. As a result, while we battle one another over a dish that is old, Little Jack Horner runs to the corner with his pudding and pie, sticks in his thumb, and pulls out a plum made of gold.

[7]
Machines 3, Angels 0

For decades the struggle for survival has included daily encounters with recalcitrant automobiles, obstinate plumbing, telephones without dial tones, and television screens with snow. Recently, at least some of us have additionally contended with user-unfriendly computers, noisy microwave ovens, and sticky tape drives on video cassette recorders. While our foremothers and forefathers wrestled with an amorphous god, we grapple with hard-edged technologies. (There are some who would say that we are still striving to put our arms around God; it's just that the contemporary one wears silicon chips instead of flowing robes.)

The difficulties created by technological innovation are not new. Generations of Mesopotamians struggled to adapt to the ecological shift from a nomadic, hunting and gathering society to a relatively settled, food-producing one. This shift, which has been termed the greatest single cultural change in human history, was made possible by experiments with food production, animal and plant domestication, and crude digging sticks, by the discovery of food preservation and storage techniques, and by the realization that sowing seeds produced crops for harvest. Most of these discoveries were undoubtedly made by women, who had been responsible for gathering the majoriity of the family diet.[1]

Millennia later, stable agricultural societies were forced to give way to a rootless Industrial Age whose development arose, again in part, from technology and invention: the steam engine, the telegraph, the cotton gin (invented by Catherine Littlefield Greene in 1793; Eli Whitney receives historical credit for it because eighteenth-century women weren't allowed to obtain patents). Even though the temptation to claim unique suffering is great, we might find it hard to prove that our transition from the Industrial to the Information Age is any more severe than what our predecessors underwent. This last transition, too, has been brought about through technology and invention: radio, nuclear fission, the transistor, the silicon chip, and the replication of DNA (for our understanding of which only James Watson and Francis Crick are acknowledged, not Rosalind Franklin[2]).

The Great Chain of Being

Traumatic shifts from one age to another were accompanied by corresponding, and no less traumatic, shifts in the philosophical evaluation of the place of human beings in the universe. Drawing on Plato's and Aristotle's conceptions of the universe, medieval theologians—Neoplatonists to the core—described a scheme called "the Great Chain of Being," which was accepted from the Middle Ages until the end of the eighteenth century by philosophers and scientists alike. According to this scheme, God created a continuous hierarchy of creatures, placing a string of animal life, from bugs to beasts, at the bottom, with the angels, archangels, and God at the top, and man (specifically male) in the middle, where body and soul were joined.[3] Poet Alexander Pope summarized the concept well:[4]

> Vast chain of being! which from God began,
> Natures aethereal, human, angel, man,
> Beast, bird, fish, insect, what no eye can see,
> No glass can reach; from Infinite to thee,
> From thee to nothing.

The concept of a Great Chain of Being is so appealing that, although it has long been discredited, its hierarchical description, particularly of the lower half of the scale, stubbornly resists being dislodged from the public mind. Wrong as it is, the Great Chain of Being continues to function as a contemporary metaphor.

The assumptions underlying the Great Chain of Being have

Figure 7.1 The Scale of Nature from Didacus Valades, *Rhetorica Christiana*, 1579, one of many variations on the Great Chain of Being (*The British Library C.107.e3*)

undergone repeated revision with each new great scientific discovery. First, Copernicus's discovery in 1543 that the heavens do not revolve about the earth, but rather that the earth revolves about the sun, stimulated questions that led to Giordano Bruno's depiction of a decentralized, infinite, and infinitely populated universe (1586).[5] Man had to move down a notch in his own estimation, and in Descartes's: "It is not at all probable that all things have been made for us in such a way that God had no other end in view in making them."[6] Newton's elucidation of the laws of motion in 1687 gave rise to the concept of the universe as a great grandfather clock, whose mechanism, wound up at creation, ticked away without either God or mortal remembering to wind it every evening. Down another notch.

Darwin's publication of the theory of evolution in *Origin of Species* in 1859 only made things worse; men might still consider themselves comfortably superior to beasts, but, horror of horrors, they had evolved from them. And by the turn of the century, Freud took even that comfort away: human beings behave instinctively; they have hidden animal urges that make their superiority questionable at best. As they slid closer and closer to the animal end of the Great Chain of Being, humans slipped further and further from the right hand of God. Well, at least the material world stayed put; if only they could catch their breath, men might at least be able to retain a thread of dominance over external events.

Wrong again. Einstein's theory of special relativity in 1905 turned the universe into a matter of perception; nothing is constant except the speed of light. Human beings were further diminished to "mere matter" when the secrets of DNA, the carrier of genetic codes in all species, were unraveled in 1953, making the human species just another recipe in a great chemical cookbook. Continuing efforts with genetic manipulation and reproductive engineering ("Immaculate Conception Bears Fruit in Glass Womb" the headlines will scream . . .) may make human beings, particularly women, extraneous even to their own survival. The very definition of life has been thrown into question.

The last stronghold of Fortress Human has been the intelligent mind; plants and animals can't "think;" things can't "think." But now that, too, is under siege by computer scientists, from Norbert Wiener, originator of cybernetics, to Stephen Wozniak, engineering designer of the Apple computer.

Maintaining the illusion

Male human beings, who for many centuries were the only ones allowed enough education to be aware of what was happening, did not take their demotion meekly. Ever resilient and resourceful, men have expended enormous effort to maintain some semblance of the Great Chain of Being and assure themselves a secure footing on the center rung. First, in order to salvage an aura of superiority, new divisions were introduced into this tacit, cultural metaphor. The Great Chain of Being took on a new look, with women and minorities appearing on the scale below men, just a mere fraction above the animals. As early as AD 581 the Church declared that women had neither souls nor reason,[7] thus making it impossible for females to provide, as males did, the crucial middle link between sentient creatures and infinite perfection. More than one eighteenth-century writer made the ranking within the human species explicit:[8]

> Animal life rises from this low beginning in the shellfish . . .
> to the confines of reason, where, in the dog, the monkey,
> and chimpanzee, it unites so closely with the lowest degree
> of that quality in man, that they cannot easily be
> distinguished from each other. From this lowest degree in
> the brutal Hottentot, reason, with the assistance of learning
> and science, advances, through the various stages of human
> understanding, which rise above each other, till in a Bacon
> or a Newton it attains the summit.

With its insistence that every living creature had its proper station in the order of things, the Great Chain of Being also offered political theorists of the late eighteenth century a minor metaphysical apology for the status quo in religion, power relationships, and the economy.[9] Again, the poet Pope summarized the position:[10]

> Order is Heav'n's first law; and this confest,
> Some are, and must be, greater than the rest,
> More rich, more wise

Craniologists in the nineteenth century and some socio-biologists in the twentieth, still seeking to convert the Great Chain of Being "from cosmological generalization to moral imperative," would labor mightily to prove that white men are superior to someone or something besides cockroaches.[11] (In terms of survival, cockroaches win.) Later, implications of both the Great Chain of Being and the theory of evolution would be transposed into Social Darwinism to justify the fact that some men attain higher class status than others, even if their DNA is the same.

In their most recent, and perhaps most desperate, attempt to preserve their shreds of status, men have sought to place "intelligent" machines (robots and computers) on an equal footing with themselves, lest the machines end up above them, closer to the angels and God. Most explicitly, *Time* magazine named the computer "Man of the Year" for 1982.[12] A year later three youths shot the brains out of a school computer forty-eight times because it "snitched" on their truancy records; the identification is apparently complete.[13]

Many manufacturers now seek to give machines that most unique of human capabilities—speech. It *is* easier for people to use computers that appear to "listen," "talk," and "understand," since machines should adapt to people, not the other way around. But when computerized automobiles badger us that the oil pressure is too low or the engine temperature too high; when grocery check-out stands start rattling off prices; when car horns yell at pedestrians and alarm clocks yodel, we must ask if talking machines haven't already said too much. (To their credit, consumers refused to buy a microwave oven with the gift of gab and Mitsubishi Electric had to stop producing its Panasonic and Quasar brand talking ovens.) If we don't make a clear distinction between talking machines and human beings, we may find ourselves emulating doll-makers who, struggling for new gimmicks, started to make dolls that wet and dirtied their diapers.

This effort to "personalize" the computer, built by male

engineers in their own image, is not a joke; they may truly be intended to reinforce men's ill-deserved aggrandizement of power. In 1983 William Shaffer, spokesman for Micro-electronics and Computer Technology Corporation (MCC), a consortium coordinating super-computer research by twelve major US companies, described his idea of the vocal computer nirvana that awaits. "I can envisage a day," he said, "when a housewife walks in the kitchen and starts getting nagged by the toaster and the refrigerator. The microwave will be waiting for the Canadian bacon and the refrigerator will be reminding her that there's food in there waiting to be cooked."[14] The first bumpersticker that asks, "Have you talked to your stove today?" should be ripped to shreds by hordes of angry women.

The idea that the computer could so threaten man's position in the Great Chain of Being that it must be co-opted to "play on (his) team" is primarily a creation of the male-dominated media. Of course, since people behave on the basis of what they *believe* to be "true" or real, it is beliefs (and therefore the media, the propagator of modern myth), not reality, that count.[15] Computers are widely perceived as a ticket on the monorail to "Tomorrowland." One television commercial even portrays a downcast youngster telling his parents he flunked out of college because he didn't have a Commodore computer. This outrageous appeal to parents' fear for their children's success is only the most blatant of the exhortations equating computer literacy with survival. These messages are intended to persuade people that they can't expect to get by on their own brains, talents and interpersonal abilities in the future: no computer skills, no job. A moment's reflection shows that what's really going on here is the establishment of a self-fulfilling prophecy: it is corporations, government, employers, schools, media and other man-made institutions that turn the computer into a meal ticket and a survival skill; it's not the "computers" doing it.

In the process of creating this new "need," we are further encouraging people to believe in their own incompetence. The decline in self-confidence is reinforced by media fascination with artificial intelligence and "expert" software that mimics human decision-making capabilities. This type of software attempts to "teach" the computer to think, reason, deduce, communicate, analyze and explain. The sheer popular appeal of chess matches between computers and master players, of the pseudo-psychoanalytic program Eliza,[16] and of "expert" programs in geological exploration, medical diagnosis and business management indicates a rather masochistic desire to deflate the capabilities of the human mind.

"Expert" programs are particularly tantalizing, not only because they are the newest attempt to apply the theories of artificial intelligence, but because they ignore a particularly human, and apparently inimitable quality: common sense. Hubert Dreyfus, a critic of "expert" programs, notes that the emphasis on applying general rules, which sits at the core of these programs, is actually contrary to reports by managers, doctors, or geologists who talk about having a "gut feeling," a "sixth sense," or just a "sense of the right thing to do" when making a critical decision.[17] Since we can't program computers to display intuition developed through years of experience, we deny its value. Perhaps the possibility of doing away with intuition and insight is attractive because these qualities have always been associated with women.

Robots, which pose a dual threat to men's shaky foothold on the Great Chain of Being, must also be co-opted. Robots are able to do things that men can't do (work in dangerous environments, for example), but cannot do things that women can (housework). A variety of single-task, industrial robots have been developed to operate in hazardous job situations; they can manipulate radioactive elements, dispose of bombs, or spray-paint metal in spite of toxic fumes. One robotics consultant doesn't want to stop there. "Robots will be even more salable," claims Elliott Wilbur of Arthur D. Little Inc. (a research and consulting firm), "if they replace skilled workers as well as low-priced laborers."[18] (Robots are already being used to shear sheep in Australia.) Better still, robots "do not take breaks, get sick, become bored, have 'blue' Mondays, take vacations or need retirement plans."[19] (Nor do they vote for a union.) Altogether superior to the male worker, right? Oops! Such acknowledgment would elevate robots over men, and therefore force men down another rung on the ladder of creation.

The difficulty of designing robotic devices that can handle

Figure 7.2 Artificial intuition (© *1982 by Sidney Harris*. What's So Funny About Computers?, *William Kaufmann, Inc., Los Angeles, California*)

women's household chores poses another threat. (From a robot's point of view, housework is quite complex because the varied chores demand multiple sensing devices and continual reprogramming.)· Maybe domestic robots will only be able to perform such "odious" repetitive chores as "cleaning the bathtub or reading a toddler's favorite story over and over."[20] (Would you let a robot read *your* child a bedtime story?) Since robots can't handle women's complex tasks, should men be placed below robots and women above?

To avoid such a result, men place the machine at their own level, claiming that it makes a perfect emotional companion. A robot (male) is "a someone, not a something—a friend that would greet you after a long day at the office," insists Nolan Bushnell, founder of Androbot Inc. which produces a "pal" called Topo.[21] And here, at last, is a way to prove that robots are superior to women: the robot makes no demands; the robot is always willing to listen; the robot is always predictable, always controllable. Ah, the perfect mate for an engineer!

For manufacturers seeking to create artificial versions of themselves, a robot—as an equal to men—should be treated with respect, not contempt. (That degree of sensitivity has never been shown to women and minorities.) The anthropomorphic form and intent of robots like Topo and Hubot (see Figure 7.3) is so successfully communicated that professors at Carnegie Mellon University choreographed a dance for a robot and a woman, and children in one family demanded that an extra plate be set for Topo at the dinner table.

Given their own attitude of respect, robotics engineers cannot fathom why other men who are directed, supervised, watched, and regulated all day might abuse a robot slave. (Much better, though, for a man to order around his robot than his wife; certainly better than turning her into an automaton-like Stepford wife. And robots are definitely preferable targets for violent anger than women, children and animals.)

Reducing the human essential

Nowhere is the loss of human uniqueness more apparent than in the fields of reproductive and genetic engineering, which seek to create new life and new life forms. Genetic engineering, under the pretense of turning man into God as the next creator, actually does the opposite: it turns God into man, trivializing the process of evolution. In one recent case, researchers mingled the embryos of a goat and a sheep to produce a "geep," claiming that their experiments would make it easier to rear embryos of endangered species in the wombs of other animals.[22] (Such hybrids are called chimeras.)

Ever since the US Supreme Court certified the patentability

"OK Gail. Call you at 10."

Introducing Hubot. The first home robot that's a personal companion, educator, entertainer, and sentry... and he can talk! **Hubot is smart.** He can talk to you with a 1200 word vocabulary. Simply choose the words and sentences that you want Hubot to use and he can greet friends, talk to your family—even wake you in the morning. Soon Hubot will be able to talk to you in your very own voice through the magic of voice synthesization.

As smart as Hubot is, he can help teach kids math, spelling, and reading with special educational programs such as Logo, which are readily available. Hubot is fun to learn from.

Hubot also has a powerful computer. It's as powerful as any you can buy separately, with a large 128K memory, disk drive, a 12" video display, simple-to-use keyboard, printer, and programs that let you quickly learn how to use a computer. Hubot is truly your personal computer.

Hubot is very mobile. Hubot can easily move around the house. His rotating OSP™ sonar collar locates obstacles so he can avoid them. You can teach Hubot the entire floor plan of your home so he can move to any room of your house. Hubot can be a companion whenever you are at home.

And when you are not at home, Hubot can act as a sentry to guard your valuable possessions. He can even detect heat and smoke to make your home safer.

Hubot is versatile. Hubot does so many things, you will never run out of ways to have fun with him. Soon available with an articulator arm, Hubot will be able to serve drinks, open doors, vacuum, and perform light household chores.

With the Smart Servant™ module, Hubot will become "the intelligent appliance for the 80's"—able to control all the electrical devices in your home: turning lights on and off, regulating temperature and energy consumption.

Hubot will always offer something new. Hubot is designed to be expandable. The Hubot you buy now is the Hubot you will have tomorrow. That's because you can add features as you desire. Hubot will always be able to do more and you can continue to enjoy him for years to come.

Buy Hubot and have your own personal fun companion. Hubot is available in fine stores everywhere. *Hubot*

Figure 7.3 Men only assume their presence is essential to women; they, too, can be replaced with robots (*Michael N. Forino, founder and president of Hubotic; inventor of Hubot*)

of new life forms in 1980,[23] the race has been on to make a fortune by producing oil-eating bacteria, cancer-consuming interferon, disease-free tomatoes and frost-resistant potatoes.

It is one thing for scientists to use recombinant DNA (gene-splicing) techniques in the laboratory; it is quite another to introduce genetically altered bacteria into the outside world, playing what author Jeremy Rifkin calls "ecological roulette." Once released into the environment, these bacteria cannot be called back if they reproduce and spread; they could change the pattern of photosynthesis, upset the ecosystem, or even disturb worldwide weather patterns.[24] Man, it appears, cannot masquerade successfully as either God or Nature.[25]

When techniques for manipulating human genes through cloning, prenatal genetic screening for desirable traits, or DNA repair *in vivo*, reach the point that they can be combined with the ability to maintain a pregnancy in an artificial environment (presently, about half of intrauterine growth can be supported outside the womb), we will be confronted with even further diminution of the species *homo sapiens*. A more "perfect" human being created in a laboratory may be considered superior to ordinary people, while "inferior" individuals may be deliberately engineered as a caste of slave laborers. (This possibility chillingly updates Hitler's conception of Aryan supremacy with "better" techniques than those available to his eugenic breeding program; the same results may be achieved, only this time with the "best of intentions," rather than the worst.)

The devaluation of human beings arises from two sources: the decreasing amount of control individuals possess over their environment, and, concomitantly, the declining importance accorded human experience in the world. Other technologies besides computers and robotics contribute to this devaluation (not always deliberately) by destroying people's confidence in their own intelligence, abilities, or creative skills.

Television programming, which is alternately described as programming for the "least common denominator" or "the least objectionable show," is a trite example of how we use technology to insult human intelligence. To say, as the networks constantly do, that we "get the programming we deserve—and want" ignores the simple reality of profit in a commercial system. The networks in the United States need to deliver the largest, demographically stratified audiences possible to their advertisers (people, not programs, are the product of television[26]). Naturally, everyone involved in this expensive proposition wants to secure their profit margins with the least possible risk. Thus, dramatic mini-series rely on trite but proven formulas, and the same inbred group of people is continually hired to supply creative and production talent to the networks.

A viewer spinning the channel selectors does *not* have "freedom of choice;" she or he can choose only from what is already there. The many technologies of television, which comprise broadcast, cable and satellite transmission, video-cassette and videodisc player/recorders, teletext and videotex, remote control, color, flat-wall and large-screen video projectors, special effects, and computer-generated graphics, are an industry unto themselves. But they say nothing about content; that decision is made by men, not machines.

The relationship of people to their architecture is another, but less common, example of the same phenomenon. The cookie-cutter cells of suburban housing developments, public housing and monster skyscrapers attempt, with varying degrees of success, to equate human habitats with those of ants and bees. The regimentation is more pronounced in business, where "personalizing" a workspace with plants and pictures is considered suspect, than it is with homes and apartments, where general messiness and an unquenchable need to make a visible statement about their identities lead people to individualize their living space over a period of years.

Personalization must arise from the enormous variety of the human endeavor; it is defeated by a machine randomly saying, "chimney on the left here, chimney on the right there," or "green walls, brown walls, yellow walls, blue walls." Columnist and commentator Ellen Goodman noted the irony of computer-controlled differentiation in a television interview about the "Cabbage Patch" doll hysteria at Christmas 1983.[27]

Perhaps mass-produced individuality will become the 1980s' answer to the mass-produced conformity of the 1950s. Even while artist Andy Warhol uses the precision and multiplicity of industrial products, such as Campbell's Soup, to make a joke about conformity, merchandisers convert the same concept into products that act as ubiquitous advertisements, from Coca

87

Cola keyrings to Big Mac pencil sharpeners.

Or consider the increasing potential of physical household management via computer. Microprocessor-controllers can water the lawn, brew coffee, turn on heating or air conditioning, rotate solar panels, flick off lights when a room is empty, roast a chicken, yell "fire," and warn off burglars. They can be installed in various appliances, from microwave ovens to videocassette recorders, be driven by a home computer, or be connected to outside systems such as burglar alarms, smoke detectors and telephones. Xanadu, the most advanced model of such a house, is located in Florida, near Disney Enterprises' EPCOT, Experimental Prototype Community of Tomorrow.[28] When the late animator Walt Disney first envisioned EPCOT, he imagined a small, futuristic town inhabited by people living real lives. As now operated, EPCOT Center is a commercial adjunct to the massive Disneyworld amusement park. No people live in it and no one would want to, which is perhaps the point. (Compare this with Williamsburg, Virginia, a restored colonial town and tourist center, inhabited year-round by 5,100 people.)

Such sensational architectural exercises may presage yet another devaluation of human status on the Great Chain of Being, since they turn over individual control of the immediate environment to a machine, just as large-scale environmental concerns, like pollution and energy production, are already removed from individual control. As Hubotics founder Michael Forino puts it, "The factory and the office have been automated, and now it is time to turn our attention to the home."[29] Taken separately, many control devices offer convenience to a working woman (turning on an oven to cook dinner at a predetermined time), energy savings (adjusting heating and air conditioning systems to reach a preset temperature just before people wake up or return home),

Figure 7.4 Xanadu is hyped as "a house you can talk to . . . a house that is also a servant, counselor and friend to every member of your family."[30] What, pray tell, are the people in this house doing? (*Reprinted with permission from* Xanadu *by Roy Mason* et al. *Copyright © 1983 by Acropolis Books Ltd, 2400 17th St NW, Washington, DC 20009; photograph by Grady Allred*)

In XANADU did Kubla Khan, a stately pleasure dome decree:
—*Coleridge*

Here Now!

XANADU

The Computerized Home of Tomorrow and How It Can Be Yours *TODAY!*

Roy Mason with Lane Jennings and Robert Evans —— Interview with Bob Masters, *Creator of Xanadu*

How your home can be an Electronic Cottage

published by **ACROPOLIS BOOKS**, Washington, D.C.

Figure 7.5 Colonial Williamsburg is promoted as a place where "taverns alive with music and laughter wake the memories of the past, while . . . artisans, craftsmen, scholars and performing artists recapture the beauty of the eighteenth century."[31] Both Xanadu and Williamsburg are commercial enterprises selling a lifestyle, but the lifestyles they sell are quite different (*Williamsburg Area Chamber of Commerce*)

reassurance (ringing the fire station automatically if a fire starts while no adult is home), or services not previously available (recording preselected television programs automatically). However, taken together they also produce potentially serious invasions of privacy and generate an illusion of progress, both because many of these "conveniences" are already available with simple clock timers and because someone still needs to bathe the baby, pull the weeds, and put coffee in the percolator, whether you have a digital or clock ("analog!") model.

The subliminal messages beneath home control units are fourfold: (1) you must give up privacy to get protective services from the state; (2) you have no right to complain about minor inconveniences because new technology has made your life "easier;" (3) you must live so predictably and rigidly that you don't get home before the heater turns on, don't go out to dinner on the spur of the moment after the casserole has started cooking, and don't decide to sleep late after the coffee has started perking (imagine trying to remember all those times if you want to change them by dialing up the machine on the telephone . . .); and (4) machines are more reliable than people. (This last message is counter-intuitive; for several years one common office sign has read "To err is human; to really screw things up takes a computer.") Taking these factors into consideration, home controllers seem to be matter of dubious progress indeed.

All technologies that affect our estimation of ourselves and our sense of uniqueness alter the subtle social construction of just how important we think we really are in the grand scheme of things. They all raise questions about access to and control over technology; they all should make us ask who benefits by the process of manipulating others through technology, and who gets ahead when people convince themselves that they haven't got as much to offer the world as a robot with a computer for a brain.

PART II

The Invisible Tyranny of Things

[8]

Progress as product

It is not enough to examine the consequences of new technology, serious as they may be, in terms of our relationships to ourselves, each other, the community, the state, the world, and the universe. If we wish to alter the course of technological development to obtain a different set of results, we must also examine the reasons technology has developed the way it has. Are the design and intent of technology as inevitable as they are made to appear? If not; if there is no truth behind the myth of technological determinism, and if there is no actual conspiracy (and I do not believe there is) to drive technology along a particular path of change, why do so many technological "advances" seem to converge on the same, not particularly desirable, set of results: alienation, coldness, depersonalization, devaluation of the female, dehumanization, increasing distance between the worker and her tools?

Which comes first: the reality of the technology or the idea of what that technology will achieve? Or is there a more complicated, dialectical relationship, instead of a cause-and-effect one, between an idea and the tangible form it takes? Can we take hold of tomorrow by changing technology, without changing the ideas behind it? What happens if we change only the ideas, without changing technology too? In our society, which, not accidentally, treasures the mind over the hands, the women's movement is greatly tempted to believe that changing such value-laden systems as the law, education, wage structures and the media will suffice to bring about lasting social change.

The problem with this approach is that the far less malleable reality of material objects presents the real obstacle to change. Forcing a company to accept affirmative action goals is a ringing achievement, but if there is no way for women without cars to get to work, it is also a meaningless one. Requiring schools to ensure that women receive an equal amount of computer education is superb, but computer communications systems that devalue women's socialized, nonverbal communications skills make that requirement absurd. In such ways, technology can unravel the skein of social change that women have been spinning and winding, with patience and at great cost, for decades.

Even in its less hostile incarnation as a passive barrier, technology presents more than just a challenge for nimble feet or muscular upper arms. The dimensions of a kitchen, the height of a lectern, the distance between the seat and steering wheel of a car all embody expectations about who will use the technology; the route of a highway, the services available by phone, the data in a database all embody implicit assumptions about what (and whose) purposes technology will serve. Since new technology is usually expensive, access to it is inevitably determined by class: a single mother working as a secretary may have greater need for a mircowave oven than a two-income professional family with live-in help, but she is much less likely to have one. In these ways new technology does more than simply reflect existing economic disparity; it embeds that disparity into new tools, products, objects and advertisements, endlessly expanding the inertial mass that must be pried into motion before change can occur.

The visible dangers of high technology—invasion of privacy, nuclear weapons, toxic wastes—receive plenty of attention. But daily-use technologies—roads and houses, telephones and television, appliances and automobiles—do as much, if not more, insidious damage by diminishing opportunities for social mobility, equity, and power-sharing, and by encasing dominant power relationships, sometimes quite literally, in concrete. Invisible because of their "ordinariness," day-to-day technologies have become so ingrained in our lifestyle we forget that, unlike pine trees and turtles, they are not part of the process of natural evolution. Someone designed these technologies, someone built them, someone sold them, and someone else uses them. Why do we forget?

The commercialization of the future

In the less self-conscious decade of the 1950s, the business of technology was brash and bold and unashamed. The then-new medium of television trumpeted a vision of a future ceaselessly improved by technology, brought to us by companies only too happy to blow their own horns. "What's good for General Motors is good for America." "Better living through chemistry," exclaimed DuPont. "Progress is our most important product," intoned General Electric. Americans, celebrating the victory of democracy over the forces of evil, settled smugly into a suburbanized "best of all possible worlds" that Voltaire's Dr. Pangloss would have envied.[1] Businesses billed technology as the only train to tomorrow and Americans kept reserving their seats: an all-electric house, a power lawnmower, a new car (with fins to get there in style), a dishwasher, a stereo record player, a self-defrosting refrigerator, a color television. "All aboard!"

But it was, and is, a train that never arrives. With every ticket we buy, the farther we are from our destination: a solar hot water heater, a new car (with a diesel engine to get there on less fuel), a cordless telephone, a videocassette recorder, a computer. Mellow woodwinds and soft strings have replaced the fanfare of brasses and horns in the commercials. General Electric now "brings good things to life." ITT smugly announces that "the best ideas are the ideas that help people." Champion Forest Products assures us "the future is coming." Security Pacific Bank is "looking forward" to it. Conglomerate TRW doesn't bother with selling a means to get there; it is "bringing us tomorrow," directly. (Mobil Oil minces no words: "More now.")

What we are buying is not, of course, tomorrow. We are buying status with solar panels, security with burglar alarm systems, distraction from the ever-present fear of nuclear war through big-screen TVs. We are buying—or trying to buy—computer insurance for our children's success, and cloned

How an idea in yesterday's funny papers can become tomorrow's financial headlines.

Dick Tracy's wrist radio used to belong strictly in the Funnies.

But a revolution in electronics is moving ideas like these onto the business and financial pages of the newspaper.

Thanks to super microchips made of a semi-conducting compound called gallium arsenide.

These miniature integrated circuits work ten times faster than conventional silicon chips.

And at higher frequencies in smaller spaces. Which could make possible satellite phone calls from personal wrist phones.

And night vision devices for crime detection that are thousands of times more efficient than the human eye.

Considering what silicon chips did for the electronics industry and Wall Street, gallium arsenide holds great promise.

One analysis projects the U.S. market for gallium arsenide integrated circuits will grow from $103 million to nearly $1.8 billion over the next nine years.

One company is building a multimillion dollar research center to develop new applications for gallium arsenide.

The company? ITT.

We're investing in the future. What are you investing in?

For current news about ITT Corporation, phone toll free 1-800-DIAL ITT for a continuously updated recorded message.

ITT

Figure 8.1 ITT: the best ideas are the ideas that help people (©
1984, ITT Corporation, 320 Park Avenue, New York, NY 10022.
Reprinted by permission: Tribune Company Syndicate, Inc.)

immortality. It's a very profitable business, this: selling a "better" future to people who are terrified they won't live to see it. We aren't really buying quadraphonic digital tape recorders, wristwatch TVs, or talking clocks; we are buying "better."

In the 1950s "better" was a fabricated virtue that existed (or so we were told) in the product, in the "better" refrigerator door, the "better" butter. In the 1980s, "better" has become an intrinsic virtue of time: "tomorrow will be better" just because it's tomorrow, not today. "Progress," a concept that had to be sold as part of a product before, is now accomplished through the inevitable rotation of the earth on its axis, one day sliding smoothly into another, "better" tomorrow. Ah, what a sly and brilliant notion! "Progress" is out of our hands; "better" is the music of the spheres! By accepting this new definition of "better," we have lost track of what "better" means; we have no way of distinguishing that "better" may be better for some than for others, since "tomorrow" happens to us all, unless we die.

Technology becomes not the means to "better," but the tangible proof that "better" has arrived. In this revisionist version of a future that is yet to be, no one is responsible for technology; no human hand, no human head can be held accountable. We buy self-improvement classes and job re-training courses so we will be worthy of a "better" future, not to create one. If, by some mischance, tomorrow seems worse instead of better, we have no one to blame for our fate but ourselves; we weren't ready. Under the cover of the myth of "better," technology is designed, produced, and marketed by companies who have something to gain and even more to protect, only we aren't aware of it any more. Like the myths of self-sufficiency, neutrality and freedom of choice, the myth of "better" has been invented.

The invention of the future

Inevitably, the question arises: why would anyone bother to invent a myth of "better" that focuses attention and effort on the future instead of the present? A quick look at the history

99

of religion may provide an answer. The Catholic Church of the late Middle Ages promised generous worshippers "life everlasting" in exchange for cash. In its practice of selling indulgences (forgiveness for sins), the Church literally sold tickets to paradise. For people in the Middle Ages, a time of constant war, plague and poverty, the promise of a better life after death was irresistible. By focusing attention on a glorious afterlife, the Church not only distracted its worshippers from the despair of their own circumstances, but also diverted their human and financial resources from local social and political activities to the Church's own benefit.

Now, with technology joining the ranks of new religions, the situation is not so different. Once again, we are distracted from the present, and rivet our attention on a future we may not live to enjoy, no matter how much we pay for it. In the meantime, those who are in power are able to set policies and institutionalize practices that will guarantee them the same degree of control over tomorrow that they exert today. Those who muse, predict and prognosticate about the future also end up definining, developing and determining it. We can hardly be surprised when the future ends up matching their descriptions of it.[2] The prophecies of futurists, futurologists and forecasters (almost all white males) are fulfilled more often than those of psychics, palm readers and fortune tellers, not because their prophecies are any more accurate, but because the futurists, futurologists and forecasters are employed by institutions powerful enough to "make their dreams come true." After all, the future is too important to be left to chance.[3]

Those dreams, almost inevitably male-centered, ethnocentric and imperialistic, reflect the interests of the institutions—government, corporations, universities, consulting firms and "think tanks"—that hire the dreamers, be they political scientists, writers, economists, military strategists, urban planners or scientists. In fact, futurism has nearly become an institution of its own.[4] Journals have proliferated rapidly; the membership of the World Future Society, the largest of the futures organizations, has expanded in less than twenty years from several hundred to 30,000 worldwide (only 20 percent are women); the number of professional prognosticators has increased until they have created their own academic discipline; but almost nowhere are women dreamers or women's issues represented.

In the late 1960s, Arjay Miller, former Dean of the Graduate School of Business at Stanford University, proposed a National Goals Institute to provide futures research to Congress and the Executive Branch of government. One of the men who attended a planning session for the institute in August 1970, James Gavin of Arthur D. Little Inc., was appalled: "Here was a large group discussing the future of goals in our society . . . and . . . there wasn't a black or a woman in the room."[5]

Many of the techniques used in modern futures research grew out of systems analysis methods that were first developed by "think tanks" for the purpose of strategic military planning. Consequently, both the techniques and the results they produce are imbued with the assumptions, values and biases of the military. "What if?" scenarios, favored by the Hudson Institute, imply, in spite of historical proof to the contrary, that it is possible to forecast events accurately. The Rand Corporation's widely used Delphi forecasting technique, which solicits rounds of opinions by "experts" until consensus is reached, assumes that the assessment of problems and selection of experts is neutral and value-free. Trend extrapolation, cross-impact analysis, and simulation modeling all rely on the mathematical manipulation of quantifiable data that is presumed to be complete, accurate and sufficient.[6]

Military thinking is replete with assumptions about the inevitability of hierarchical power relationships, the superiority of Western industrial methods, and an optimistic faith in the ability of technology to solve all problems. And, of course, those who forecast the future, be they academicians or authors, social scientists or military strategists, have a vested interest in seeing that their prophecies are fulfilled. No phrase massages the male ego quite so effectively as the self-stroking "I told you so." With this background, it is no wonder that the solutions look so much like the problems!

"Think tanks" like the Rand Corporation, the Institute for the Future in Menlo Park, SRI International (formerly the Stanford Research Institute), the Brookings Institute, and the

Hudson Institute founded by the late Herman Kahn (perhaps the best-known futurist, famous for his authorship of numerous studies about thermonuclear war) are a unique postwar contribution to the invention of the future. These institutes, which receive millions of dollars in corporate and government funding, have created a business that explicitly manufactures the idea of tomorrow. In the process, they edge out many other multiple sources of information, initiative and vision that could contribute to a collective, and perhaps more satisfactory, definition of the future.

The roots of the "think tank" concept are sunk deep in the soil of Western philosophy, reaching back in history to Plato's academy in 387 BC. For Plato, rational thinking was all-important; only through the mind could the world be known and understood. The Academy, like the other cultural and educational institutions of the ancient Greeks, was open only to free men: no slaves or women allowed. (Plato had espoused the theoretical equality of women in both the *Republic* and the *Laws*, but he backed away from this position in practice, finding it essential to socialize women differently so they would perform their assigned domestic functions within the family.) For his successor, Aristotle, there was no conflict: Aristotle unambiguously assigned women, whose hands were sullied with the dirt of childbirth, to the material reality of daily life, while men, free of such mundane burdens, were free to explore the exalted superior region of pure thought.[7]

Like their tribal ancestors who reserved relationships with the gods for male shamans, and their Chinese contemporaries who divided the world into interactive components of male/head/yang and female/body/ying, the Greeks separated men from women on the basis of spiritual versus material. Today's "think tanks" maintain the Aristotelian tradition of excluding women's concerns and interests from the future, even if they do hire women as research assistants and secretaries.

Ecofeminists, who would link feminism and ecology based on women's "traditional" affinity with the earth and nature, reinterpret Aristotle's separation of the sexes in a hazardous manner. By grounding women in the earth and insisting on biologically based parallels between "the domination of

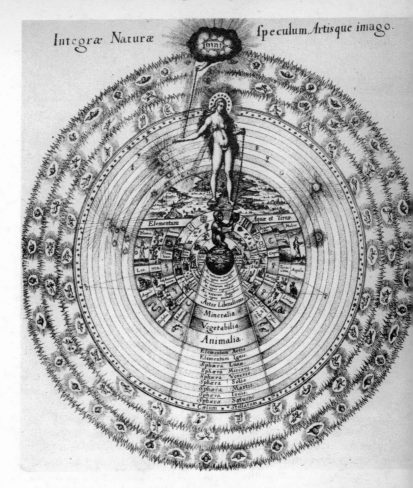

Figure 8.2 The Female Soul of the World, engraved by Johann Theodore de Bry and conceived by Robert Fludd in his *Utriusque Cosmi Maioris Scilicet et Minoris Metaphysica* (1617-21). Fludd, an alchemist, represented here the Western linkage of the right hand with masculinity, God, the sun, and dominance, and the linkage of the left hand with femininity, the earth, the moon, water, and subordinance (*Courtesy, The Bancroft Library, University of California, Berkeley*)

women and the domination of nature ... between the repudiation of the body and the despoiling of the earth," ecofeminists open women to charges that their bodies, not their minds, define their abilities.[8] "Biology is destiny" may allow lawyers to plead "premenstrual syndrome" as a defense for murder, but it also permits doctors to assert that women can't think when they have their periods. Whether it comes from men or women, from ecofeminists or the military, an artificial division between the mind and the body ends up divorcing women from the manipulation of ideas and, ultimately, from participating in efforts to think about the future we want to have.

Although Western philosophy has constrained women's domination to the practical, the material, or the dirty, women are still not the "queens of things" that division of territory might suggest. Since the Renaissance, male manipulation of the world of things, especially for purposes of mastery, conquest, adventure, status, or exploitation, has been constant. Women racing car drivers like Janet Guthrie, astronauts like Sally Ride, and structural engineers like the late Emily Roebling (who supervised the construction of the Brooklyn Bridge) are notable role models specifically because there are so few women who do what they have done. In general, women reign over washing machines, toilet bowls and kitchen stoves; their manipulation of the physical environment is limited to daily-use technologies that have been designed and built by men.

Philosopher Alan Watts has said that "things are the measuring units of thought just as pounds are the measuring units of weighing."[9] Grossly allotted, the "things" and tools that express creative, inventive or masterful thought—buildings, new cars, space stations—are the coin of the male-built world, while the "things" of women's world express repetitive (i.e. nonoriginal) service. (There are many specific exceptions to this general rule, such as the expressive result of women's art or the creative use of needle-and-thread as a tool. However, these tools and forms of expression are also devalued by male critics; women's art is labeled "craft" and denigrated as decorative, for instance.[10])

As long as the invention of the future, and therefore its

expression in "things," remains in the heads of white males, women's concerns will be so little regarded that women may well be left out of the future altogether. Their historical invisibility is rapidly being transformed into future invisibility; the changes wrought by the women's movement are considered nothing more than minor perturbations within a simulation game. Creating a women's vision and a women's voice for tomorrow has, so far, been left to such notable science fiction writers as Ursula LeGuin, Sally Gearhart, Joanna Russ and Marge Piercy. But they cannot be left to scream alone into the media winds. Unless many more women add their voices to the discussion, the only control women will have over the future will be to "wish upon a star."

The discussion of the future

While we pay tremendous attention to how the mass media affects our interpretation of today's issues, we too often ignore its role in bringing us the future. Popular magazines, television, radio, films and newspapers do more than shape the discussion of tomorrow; wittingly or not, they turn the invention of the future into implied consensus about its inevitability. With a few notable exceptions, media outlets do not bother to employ a staff member qualified to deal with the issues of tomorrow (there are fewer than 200 science writers for over 12,000 media outlets), so unless an issue raises obvious and vocal political dissent (e.g. toxic wastes or nuclear power), no one is available to evaluate critically what implications a scientific or technical development might have.

Instead, because of their preoccupation with the new and the different, the media adopt a "golly-gee-whiz, ain't-this-wonderful" approach to stories about scientific discoveries and technological "breakthroughs." Since editors expect the complex issues raised by science and technology to discourage writers, as well as viewers and readers, they focus on the "drama" of discovery. Also, because of the limited time or space allotted to any one story, the media rarely explore the long-term consequences of technical development or examine critical dissent within the scientific community. To most of the popular media, technology has neither history nor conflict; it exists only in the moment of its presentation. And because of their tendency to repeat and amplify the same stories, the media lend credence to tentative and, sometimes, worthless theories. If one major newspaper or wire service picks up a story, by the next day newspapers, television stations and radio programs carry the same story around the country or around the world. Errors and interpretations recur and recur, until fiction becomes fact. Without the ability, resources, interest, time or inclination to confirm such stories, people accept media interpretation as truth and base their behavior on what they've read, seen or heard.

The myths of neutrality, objectivity and progress, which cling to the silky fabric of science, intensify the power of the media. Engineers and scientists, after all, rank near the top when pollsters ask the public whom they trust. (Lawyers, politicians and car salesmen are at the bottom.) The power of the mass media is mammoth in almost every circumstance, but it has particular potency when coupled with the undeservedly virtuous reputations of science and technology. For example, in 1980 the *Los Angeles Times* ran a feature in their *Home* magazine section about the city in the year 2080. The future city is replete with solar collectors, jet scooters driven by men, and exotic skyscrapers filled with male executives, but devoid of traffic jams, smog and women.[11] Implicit in this superficially innocuous image of the future is the insidious idea that women have no role to play in it.

Or consider the enormous media attention paid to socio-biology, the latest incarnation of continual attempts to find a biologically based rationalization of the unequal status of women and minorities in society. By the early twentieth century, craniologists had given up; they hadn't been success-ful in measuring brain size: women's brains were smaller than men's, but the ratio of female brain size to body weight was larger. Try as they might, scientists were unable to develop a scale that would "prove" men were more intelligent than women. Hormonal theories replaced craniology, but they, too, lost favor when scientists discovered that both men and women had male hormones (androgens) and female hormones (estrogens) present in their bodies; it proved too difficult to correlate hormone levels and behavior.[12] But the publication in 1975 of E.O. Wilson's book *Sociobiology* revived efforts to prove that male biological superiority acounted for men's greater share of wealth and power.[13]

According to the sociobiological argument, behavior is genetically, rather than culturally or environmentally determined, and sex differences are therefore critical in deciding successfully adaptive behavior. (Women have two "X" chromosomes; men have an "X" and a "Y".) Biogenetic differences are held conveniently and totally accountable for the evolution of a higher level of male aggression and hence dominance, for the hierarchical structure of society, and for a sexual division of labor that conforms to sex-role stereotypes. Authors like Wilson and David Barash (*Sociobiology and Behavior*, 1977) assert that it is biologically impossible for the women's movement to achieve social equality between the sexes: "Mother Nature," says Barash, "appears to be a sexist."[14]

Equally offensive theories imply that men's supposedly greater abilities in math, science and logical thinking arise from hormonal programming of the brain or from sex-based differences in brain lateralization (whether the visual-spatial/intuitive right side of the brain or the analytical/verbal left side of the brain is predominant). Investigators have gone through great contortions to try to connect brain lateralization with sex-role expectations—trying to prove women are right-brain dominant and men left-brain dominant—but they have an impossible task: men are stereotyped as better at visual-spatial/analytical skills, and women at intuitive/verbal ones![15]

The media have given great play to all of these supposedly proven theories, culminating in the story of the famous "math genes," which were heralded as an explanation for why so many more men than women are scientists and engineers.[16] In 1980 the well-regarded journal *Science* published an article by Camilla Benbow and Julian Stanley, who insisted that genetic differences should be sought to explain the differences in scores between seventh and eighth grade boys and girls who took the mathematical portion of the Scholastic Aptitude Test to determine if they were mathematically gifted. Although Benbow and Stanley ignored socialization factors apart from the number of math classes students had taken and many scientists disagreed with both their data and their conclusions, newspapers and weekly magazines trumpeted the Benbow/Stanley article as proof that boys were born better at math.[17] Later, "math genes" were cited in Congressional testimony as a reason for not funding programs to increase the number of women in science.[18]

The extraordinary media attention paid to this and other stories that demonstrate biological and genetic causes for sexual, racial or class differences in behavior "ends up reinforcing social stereotypes and suggesting that our social structures are 'natural' and that we should be very careful about trying to change them," warns chemist Marian Lowe. "They reinforce sex roles and, ultimately, justify the whole power structure of society."[19] In this way, the media do much more than merely report the predictions of futurists or the discoveries of scientists. They participate actively in the invention of the future they purport to explain and, in fact, have a vested interest (only 10 percent of media workers in decision-making positions are women[20]) in maintaining a power structure as beneficial to them as it is to the scientists and engineers whose work they discuss.

[9]

What are rights without means?

When Rebecca Harding Davis described steelworkers' lives—
too circumscribed by work for the soul to breathe—in her
book *Life in the Iron Mills* in 1861, she had in mind the right
to achieve economic security.[1] What good was it to have the
"right" to be an artist or the "right" to get ahead, if wages
were so low that endless hours of work under brutal conditions
were essential just for survival? A similar irony afflicts the
relationship between economic rights and technological
means. What good does it do a woman to have the right to
work as an engineer, if she is discouraged from learning
mathematics and science in elementary school? What does it
mean to have the right to be a teamster, if she is too short to
reach both the steering wheel and the clutch in a truck? How
much can a woman really learn about computers, if she is only
told which keys to press on a word processor?

As we saw in the last chapter, material reality is a potent
force in determining social reality. Since technology embeds
existing value systems into material reality, changing people's
minds may not be enough to change their lives. Unfortunately,
changing minds—through legislation, media, or court decisions—is sometimes easier than trying to alter the route of a
railroad, the practice of *in vitro* fertilization, or the computer-
izaton of banking systems. For reasons at once obvious and
complex, changing the world of things is difficult and
expensive.

A matter of substance

In a world divided by gender, males and females, on the whole, manipulate sets of artifacts that have very different physical qualities. Men have ended up controlling objects whose persistence, scale, cost and integration with complex social systems give the objects themselves unconsidered dominance in our lives.

For instance, men have historically controlled the building of permanent monuments, from the Great Pyramid of Cheops to the Lincoln Memorial. (Three notable exceptions: Emily Roebling served as construction coordinator on the Brooklyn Bridge, which was completed in 1883; Julia Morgan, a prolific California architect, designed the San Simeon estate, finished in 1937, of newspaper magnate William Randolph Hearst; Maya Ying Lin designed the new Vietnam Veterans' Memorial in Washington, DC, in 1982 while studying architecture at Yale.[2])

Women have made major contributions to architecture, but their mud huts, tepees and bamboo shelters were either moved so frequently or replaced so regularly with new materials that women rarely received acknowledgment for their achievements.[3] Women may have invented the arch by bending saplings for a hut, for example, but it is Roman men who get credit for exploiting women's discovery. Other women, like Sophia Hayden, who designed the Woman's Building at the Columbian Exposition in Chicago in 1893, see their constructions torn down after only six months. When barely 5 percent

Figure 9.1 The few monuments that women have built are notable indeed.
(a) upper left: Vietnam Veterans Memorial, designed by Maya Ying Lin (*Dolores Neuman, photographer*);
(b) upper right: San Simeon, designed by Julia Morgan (*photograph by Walter Steilberg*);
(c) center: Brooklyn Bridge, construction supervised by Emily Roebling (*Museum of the City of New York*);
(d) bottom: Women's Building at the Columbian Exposition, designed by Sophia Hayden (*Chicago Historical Society*)

What are rights without means?

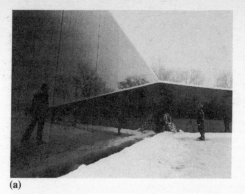

(a)

(b)

(c)

(d)

111

of American or British architects are female,[4] it is not likely that there will be many monument-builders among them.

The products of men's labor persist (sometimes even negatively so, as with toxic and radioactive wastes), but the equally important products of women's labor either decay or are consumed. From metal-tipped spears of the Bronze Age collected in museums to acres of crushed cars of the Automobile Age collected in junkyards, we see continual evidence of male-created technology; it is much more difficult to preserve the acorn meal leached of poisonous tannic acid by women of the Paiute and Kumeyaay Indian tribes in California, to excavate the mud-lined grain storage pits constructed by African women, or to display the robes that Sappho wore in ancient Greece. The female-made turkey dinner may be transitory, but the transistor surely is not.

In their ceaseless quest for prominence, men undertake large-scale projects, both to prove their own abilities ("things as a measure of thinking . . . .") and to intimidate others. Men built the Great Wall of China, the Aswan Dam, centralized electrical utilities, and communications satellites (which Professor William Melody has wryly dubbed "the ultimate professional tinkertoy"). Women invented the revolving oven, an improved washing machine, and the common clothespin (Shaker women)[5], a fan for dispensing poisonous gases (Hertha Ayrton in World War I), hair straighteners for Blacks (Sarah Breedlove "Madam C.J." Walker, the first Black woman to become a millionaire, in 1905); a belt for sanitary napkins (Black inventor Beatrice Kenner in 1956);[6] and condensed milk (Gail Borden in 1851).[7] Whereas men lay claim to objects of greater-than-human scale, women, often because of their socially restricted, domestic roles, claim mainly objects smaller than a breadbox.

Through their greater economic power, men have also managed to retain control over technologies that are expensive to implement. The relative "cost" of a technology may derive from its sacredness, as in the production of ceremonial masks of the Kono tribe in Guinea, or from the rarity of the natural resources it requires, such as the diamonds used in jewelry manufacture or the gold used to fabricate integrated circuits. By contrast, the familiarity of items in the female realm breeds contempt; precisely because pottery, cooking utensils and baskets are in daily use, they are made of common materials, inexpensive to replace if the items become dirty or broken. In many other cases, the cost of technology is related to the size and complexity of the undertaking: drilling offshore oil wells and launching spaceships cannot be accomplished with pin money. Because of their relatively high social position, men have been far more able than women to acquire and control the massive amounts of capital needed to finance research and development activities, to afford patent and legal fees, to deploy a technology and to market it aggressively.

Consequently, men have been allowed to undertake projects that integrate various public functions, such as transportation and urban planning, while women are relegated to private space. Thus, men developed subways, skyscrapers and helicopters, while women invented cut nails and the circular saw. (Both were invented in 1810 by Sarah Babbitt, known in Shaker society as Sister Tabitha; the Shakers were exceptional utopians in their appreciation of technology as the product of "consecrated brains.")[8] The effects of the steam engine, electricity, the telephone, and the assembly line (all developed by men) have reverberated throughout society, but female inventions, centered on domestic applications, have been restricted to the "unimportant" private realm.

Self-fulfilling prophecy outweighs coincidence in accounting for this apparent male monopoly over social- and life-altering inventions. Many of these inventions were adopted specifically because they were made by men; important innovations by women, such as Ann Harned Manning's improved cutting blades for a mower and reaper early in the nineteenth century, were legitimated only when a male (in this case her husband) patented them.[9] Inventions by women that might have a very different impact on social development often languish for lack of attention or financing until they become outdated, or are sold cheaply, like Ellen Eglin's clothes wringer for $18, to promoters who get rich at the inventor's expense. Eglin, who was Black, feared that white women wouldn't buy the wringer if she marketed it herself in 1888.[10]

Those cases in which women's discoveries continue to be of value or cause dramatic shifts in social structure go unremarked and unlabeled as the product of women's hands. Such is the case with the invention of what was probably the world's first tool—a sling to carry children[11]—and the discovery of horticulture by women perhaps 100,000 years ago;[12] the design, in the first century AD, by the Alexandrian alchemist Maria the Jewess of a distiller, a water bath, and other laboratory apparatus still used today; the mathematician Hypatia's invention of the astrolabe, used for celestial navigation by centuries of explorers and sailors;[13] or the discovery of the process for silk culture and weaving by the Chinese Empress Si-Ling Chi circa 2640 BC.[14] Without a doubt, Anonymous was a woman.

The very qualities of complexity, large scale, and high cost that characterize male-defined technologies enable those technologies to affect many aspects of public life simultaneously. Once a technology like computers or telephones spreads throughout the general culture, it becomes impossible to imagine living any other way. Multiple accessories, from computer software and printers to telephone directories and phone booths, are developed to take advantage of the new technology. Those with expert knowledge or a mind for opportunity quickly offer new services—programming, consulting, answering services—and create new occupations. The costs of design, manufacture and installation of a technology often can be recouped only if enormous pressure is brought to bear on consumers, who, in turn, pressure other consumers to purchase the technology as a justification of their own expenditure. (The market is much more "free" within a technological category. For example, consumers rejected the Edsel car, Bell Telephone's early Picturephone service and talking microwave ovens, but they did not reject cars, phones or microwave ovens.)

Within a relatively short period of time, many people acquire a vested interest in almost all expensive, large-scale technologies. Whether they invest in it, design it, sell it or buy it, everyone associated with a technology has a stake in seeing that it proliferates. Technological systems thus take on a logic of their own by the simple virtue of their existence: they are, therefore they must be. Reversing a technological development is nearly impossible: consider the $7 billion cost and seven-year disruption of building a new subway like the METRO in Washington, DC, to supplement inadequate roads and surface transit systems. In mature, post-industrial societies, poor technologies may be supplanted by new ones, but they cannot be repealed. We can grumble all we want about a technological system, but once it is in place, we must confront the plaint about the weather attributed to Mark Twain: "Everybody talks about [it], but nobody does anything about it."

The myth of omnipotent technology

If we accept Twain's lament as an equally accurate reflection on the futility of trying to change technology, we may as well stop right here. Forget about training women in math, science and engineering. Forget about bringing technical issues out of sedate, corporate boardrooms into the arena of noisy public debate. Forget about learning enough about sewers and computers to change the social infrastructure. Forget about altering the equation that states "them that has, gets." No one would be happier than "them that has," if we forget, throw up our hands in despair, and go back to reading novels instead of computer magazines, cultivating gardens instead of political contacts, and working out at the gym instead of at Greenham Common.

The myth of omnipotent technology, like the myth of technological determinism, functions to obscure the real people and real organizations that decide who will design new technology, who will have access to it, and who will control it; the myth masks the puppeteers. Considering the contervailing enormities of risk and profit associated with a new technology, it is not surprising that those now in control do their best to stay there. Since they realize that the rewards of success, in terms of both money and power, will be massive (far greater than the rewards women receive for taking comparable risks), and that there are equally massive losses associated with failure, they try to protect their investment. Risk minimization may take the form of refusing to expose a design to criticism, opposing government regulations necessary for health and safety, trusting only employees like themselves, i.e. white males, cutting production costs, overhead, salaries or benefits to maintain the largest possible profit margin, and keeping other fingers out of the pie.

The central fallacy of this approach lies in maximizing short-term profit at the expense of long-term benefit. A society like ours, which reduces community obligations to legal ones, lacks a feedback mechanism to encourage a longer view. For example, if a roof thatcher in medieval England had done a poor job, no one else in the village would have hired him; he would have had to face his disgruntled customer every evening in the pub and word would have spread to neighboring villages that his work was no good. Rather than blaming the quality of the thatch, the thatcher would have repaired the roof and decided it would have been better to have done a good job in the first place. But today, if a contractor builds a roof that leaks, he is subject only to damages resulting from not fulfilling his legal obligations. He may blame the quality of the shingles, i.e. the technology, and place the responsibility at someone else's door. There is no social obligation to warn a neighbor, no form of public embarrassment, no effective means of communciating the contractor's poor performance. The homeowner would end up fixing the roof or putting a pail under the leak, particularly if she or he is too poor to sue.

This trivial example illustrates several important principles. First, technology, from roofing to roto-rooting, needs to be placed within its social context. The problem is more than just a private problem of the individual with a leaking roof; it is a public problem of how we assign and enforce responsibility for the consequence of technology. Second, it has become easier to blame the technology (e.g. the roofing shingles) than to hold accountable the people involved with its production, distribution and application. Our legal system supports this approach by permitting sellers to claim that "no warranty is expressed or implied." The computer manufacturer is not liable for lost data, the electric company is not liable for inadequate power, the phone company is not liable for a contract lost because of a broken phone. Technological failures are "acts of God," not of men. The existing system appears "omnipotent," difficult to correct or modify. And finally, we totally lose track of how such a situation evolved and who actually benefits from it.

A matter of language

Not only do men benefit by designing the technology, they also benefit by determining who will control its market penetration and its insertion into the social fabric. The words "penetration" and "insertion" are used deliberately because they typify the vocabulary common in technological discourse, advertising and market research. Language itself cooperates in the myth that technological development is a "one-shot" activity that only men can perform. Linguistic issues range from the use of patently sexist words and phrases to the subtle use of the emotionless and distant passive voice. We are all conditioned to know that "hardware" is more masculine than "software," so we aren't surprised to find that women constitute less than 4 percent of all computer engineers, but nearly 30 percent of programmers.[15]

What about such superficially neutral words like "joystick"? The phallic origination of the word is usually avoided, but it sometimes slips out unnoticed in public pronouncements. According to *Time* magazine, Alan Kay, chief scientist at Atari, the videogame manufacturer, closed a June 1983 conference at Harvard University "with a vision of the video-game joy stick as a magic wand capable of creating new worlds."[16] Joysticks surely are not gender-neutral in that phrase, or in the way men hold them! Professor Edna Mitchell of Mills College found that "mothers, especially, were frustrated at not being able to make the stick do what they wanted."[17] And one engineer made the sexual connection explicit while describing a voice recognizer used by the pilot of a jet plane: "He can keep his hand on his joystick and touch the buttons with his tongue at the same time."[18]

Even setting aside blatantly sexist, racist and pornographic videogames like "Custer's Revenge," which showed a trouser-less "Custer" raping an Indian maiden tied to a stake (protests by feminist and Indian groups eventually succeeded in having production of the game discontinued; "Beat 'Em and Eat

'Em" by the same manufacturer, American Multiple Industries, however, is still being sold[19]), discussions of high-tech items are replete with sex-role stereotypes that should have been discarded long ago. In 1980, National Semiconductor demonstrated the "Digitalker," a speech synthesizer chip, by playing such sample telephone messages as a doll cooing, "I'm cute, aren't I?" A math professor speaking at a 1981 Rotary Club luncheon in Gloversville, New York, compared a computer to "a perfect wife—it cannot speak, does exactly what it's told, and works fast," and concluded that the human factor couldn't be replaced because "computers have lousy legs." Roy Mulhall, group vice-president at the California-based Uniden Corporation, boasted in 1984 that his firm's telephones are easy to use because they are designed for the lowest common denominator of under-standing—a woman's. "We simplify products under the Susie Smith concept," he explained. Sculptor Clayton Bailey exhibited his robot "Sweetheart" in a fifteenth anniversary display at the Lawrence Hall of Science in Berkeley, California, until the deputy director received numerous complaints that "Sweetheart," a silent, 5-foot coffeepot with very large breasts, degraded women.

Sexism extends to the process, as well as the products of technology. In his remarkably offensive 1982 book *Winning the Games Scientists Play*, author Carl Sindermann expended nearly twenty pages on sexist steroetypes of women in science, including, under the subheading "Sex in the laboratory," such comments as, "It is a clearly observable fact that many laboratories are peopled by significant numbers of young attractive females—sometimes by design of the director or principal investigators." Warning supervisors to avoid the complications of laboratory liaisons, he cautioned, "The very important father image, which is a reality regardless of protestations of equality, can be irrevocably shattered by even the hint of such extramarital involvement."[20] That these passages, and others like them, can be found in a recently published work, should serve notice that however far we've come, we have much farther to go before we eliminate sexism from science and technology. Even the usually sensitive and aware Apple Corporation blew its image in a mass-mailed

Figure 9.2 "Sweetheart": robot sexism (*Gary Canaparo, photographer*)

marketing letter from William Campbell, Director of Corporate Programs, who told managers how to get ahead: "don't plan to marry the president's daughter, but do plan to get an Apple."

The language of technological decision-making is as offensive as the language of technology itself. Dr. Sandra Emerson Hutchins, formerly a technical director and the highest-ranking woman in a technical field at ITT Corporation, cites such commonly used phrases as "got him by the short hairs," "got his whizzer caught in the wringer," "got him coming and going (or front and rear)," and this gem of management philosophy, "when you have them by the balls, their hearts and minds will follow." "It's no surprise," she says, "that

119

women have difficulty conquering this vocabulary or are viewed with suspicion if they do."[21]

Language does more than offend; it also excludes. Esoteric technical vocabularies become the adult male equivalent of the secret codes used to keep girls out of the boys' backyard clubhouse. Rather than clarifying communication, such codes often complicate it with legalese, bureaucratese and technologese. They function like the Mason's "secret handshake" to affirm membership in a select society and exclude those who do not belong. When combined with the passive voice, which depersonalizes language by not identifying the "subject" who performs an action, and with such euphemisms as calling a missile "The Peacekeeper," esoteric vocabularies successfully obscure the true meaning of a sentence.[22]

The mystifying, technocratic language that results not only bears unerring resemblance to George Orwell's "Newspeak," but also puts off women, whose language reflects their conditioned need to include emotional cues about acceptance, rejection, openness and love in verbal expression. It is difficult for anyone to converse in other than a native tongue. In this case, the distancing, male language of technology is discomfiting, but women's own natural style is devalued as "unscientific, imprecise, or subjective—with the again unquestioned assumption that these are *ipso facto* negative characteristics," notes linguist Robin Lakoff.[23]

Figure 9.3 "You can't play in our fort" (*SALLY FORTH by Greg Howard; Field Enterprises, Inc., 1983. Courtesy of News America Syndicate*)

This linguistic double bind has not prevented women from entering scientific and technical fields, but it has complicated their efforts to communicate effectively with their colleagues. The difficulty is compounded when men assert an exclusive right over the power of naming. From Aristotle to Linneaus to Darwin, classifying and naming objects has been a primary goal of natural history. But names are more than the convenient handles attached by an inquisitive 7-year-old struggling to make sense of the world; they impose limits and insert artificial boundaries between things, whether or not those limits or boundaries exist in nature. What is animal cannot be plant; what is male cannot be female; what was particle could not be wave, until Einstein realized that language had created a duality that the physical world did not respect. ("Duality" is more a problem in English than in Eastern languages, since our syntax constructs the word "or" as the mutually exclusive choice of "either one or the other"; Japanese interprets "or" to mean "one or the other or both simultaneously." The Japanese interpretation is equivalent to the "inclusive or" used in computer logic.)

Our ancestors had less arrogance than many of today's scientists; "Yahweh," the Hebrew word for God, was never to be spoken because naming the concept would imply a limit to the power of an omnipotent God. A name assigns intrinsic value (this is worthy of being named, that is not), connotes

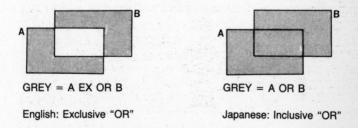

GREY = A EX OR B   GREY = A OR B

English: Exclusive "OR"   Japanese: Inclusive "OR"

Figure 9.4 These diagrams illustrate the difference between the English and the Japanese use of the word "or." It is a distinction that critically determines how we interpret the world around us.

respect ("Madonna" or "whore"), and implies certainty of knowledge ("virus" or "bacteria"). Unfortunately, names hide the identity of who does the naming, who assigns the value, who possesses the knowledge or how tentative it is, and who has the right to confer respect. Poet Susan Griffin cautions, "we did not invent the blackbird, we say, we only invented her name."[24] No wonder men guard the power of naming so jealously and resist allowing women to participate in the creation of new technologies, all of which need new names!

It may be intimidating to realize that words, as well as wealth, are accomplices in perpetuating the inequities of access to and control over technology, but this realization also explains why it is so necessary for women to be involved in every step of technological design and decision-making, from the first glimmer of an idea to the sale and use of every finished product. The power of the forces behind entrenched technology is certainly no excuse for refusing to play David to their Goliath. However, before striding out, slingshot in hand, we would do well to explore the nature of Goliath in greater depth, the better to know where the process of technological development might be vulnerable to change. With those stones from the next chapter in our pocket, we will finally be able to decide who's going to control technology and who's going to wash the dishes.

[10]
The politics of technology

Since almost every technology has a different history and operates in a different context, it is treacherous to generalize about the processes that bring technology out of the mind and into the world. Of necessity, I paint the political background of the technological canvas with broad brushstrokes, against which women's involvement, or lack of it, stands out in detail. It should be no surprise that the separate, but inseparable, procedures of science and technology—basic and applied research, innovation and invention—acquiesce in the conventional sex-role stereotypes of the larger social and economic system. In doing so, they determine how and why the design process takes place, who does it, and who will have access to and control over a technology once it reaches the marketplace. By considering three factors—the procedures of scientific investigation, the critical element of timing, and the role of government funding—we can better understand how women get shut out of the scientific and technological enterprise.

Mother Nature

According to schoolteachers' incessant drill, science progresses by rigorously testing the results of experiments against a verifiable hypothesis. Historians and philosophers often cite this procedure for teasing the truth out of nature, called the scientific method, as the crowning achievement of Western rationalism, and allege that it is superior to faith, superstition, mysticism, intuition, psychic phenomenology, and other "unprovable" ways of knowing. The dominant white male culture disparages as ignorant fools all those who contest this process or who do not "believe" a scientifically proven truth. Odd, isn't it, that truth should be a matter of belief. . . .

Disbelief and distrust, however, are the price that science must pay for its collaboration in maintaining an inequitable distribution of power and resources and in oppressing women and minorities. Scientific techniques have been used to "verify" that the minds of women are defective because menstruation weakens the supply of blood to the brain, and to "prove" that Blacks are genetically less intelligent than whites.[1] Such malevolent conclusions are not merely the result of an individual occasionally twisting the aims of science to match his own prejudice; they are an inevitable result of pretending that limited, value-laden, even sometimes irrational science has no limits, no values, and no irrationality.

Just as a particular technology comes into existence because those who develop it decide that it is important enough to produce, so, too, does science depend on scientists themselves deciding which questions are important enough to answer. Men may find it more important to research techniques for prolonging life (they generally die younger than women do) than to find a safe, reliable contraceptive. Financial and physical resources (equipment, laboratory space and graduate research assistants) are, therefore, allocated to meet male needs, extrapolated from male experience. Science is an expensive undertaking; very little of it can take place in a garage or basement any more. Physicists today work with multi-million dollar particle accelerators in specially built facilities; Marie Curie worked from 1892 to 1893 in her Parisian attic apartment. A marine biologist can still enjoy a free coastline to study tidepools, but aquanaut Sylvia Earle needs an expensive deep-sea diving suit to study fish life on the ocean floor.

Imitating the bottom-line, short-term profit mentality of business, the scientific enterprise demands numerical justification for grants given and money spent. The emphasis on quantification and measurement—how many galaxies in the universe, how many rats run a maze, how many articles are

Figure 10.1 Marie Curie at work in her laboratory (*Laboratoire Curie*)

published, how many conferences attended—conveniently supplements the naming and labeling efforts that comprise so much of scientific activity. Susan Griffin, in her book *Woman and Nature*, eloquently exposes the futile self-absorption of such activity:[2]

> He says that through numbers 1 2 3 4 5 6 7 we find the ultimate reality of things 8 9 10 11 He says 12 13 14 that quantities are the most rigorous test of things 12 13 He says God created numbers and our minds to understand numbers 14 15 16 He says the final proof 16 17 is always a sum 18 19 20. . . . *He tells us how strong he is.* He counts the sperm in his seminal fluid. He numbers his genes. . . . (She numbers the seconds. She numbers the hours. She numbers the days.) 27 28 29 30 31

In too many cases, quantification becomes an end in itself,

without regard to what is measured, how useful or valuable the measurement, how accurate the technique, or how appropriate its use. Quantification reassuringly obscures that which we do not know: in fields like psychology, where practitioners collect much data, but understand little, it is tempting to consider stacks of data as "hard" knowledge and dismiss interpretation as "soft." The computer, by making quantification easier, has also made it more prevalent, even for absurd applications.

For instance, *Human Edge Software* sells a "Sales Edge" program for $250 that purports to provide a psychological profile of customers so marketers can adjust their "pitch" to match the prospect's style. Not too surprisingly, female sales workers have been much more skeptical than their male colleagues about relying on computers to establish rapport with a client.[3] The trust that men place in such systems can be seriously abused; some employers accept computerized psychological tests as a means of determining an applicant's suitability for employment, and some courts consider the tests adequate to determine sanity and the ability of a defendant to stand trial.

The stress on quantifiable data promotes the illusion that while qualitative data are subjective, quantity is pure; it conceals the role of intuition in scientific discovery and technical achievement. Measurement reduces the truly exciting aspects of science to the figures they produce. The insights required to construct the hypothesis and design the experiment, to figure out which questions to ask and how to find the answers, dissolve in the resulting mass of data. Consequently, the "guess" is one of the best kept secrets of science. In what is surely one of the most creative exercises in revisionist history, most men depict a successful scientific endeavor as the culmination of thinking that is clear and cautious, while heaping sarcasm on the possibility that "irrational" insight contributed to their success. (Only the most exceptional scientists have enough ego security to admit, as did Nobel Prize-winning physicist Richard Feynmann, that a 6-year-old child playing in the school yard could solve problems he could not.)

The vehement denial of intuition arises, most probably,

from the fear that admitting intuition would be tantamount to admitting women into the sacred ranks of scientists at the very highest level. The irony is obvious: women, stereotyped as intuitive, emphatic, unpredictable, patient, practical and persevering, have an absolutely superb set of qualifications for science and invention. Barbara McClintock, Nobel Prize winner for Physiology and Medicine in 1983, thanked her subject, maize, for solving problems for her.[4] Inventor and artist Frances GABe, builder of the Self-Cleaning House in Newburg, Oregon, fueled her creative solutions with a raging insistence that "there had to be a better way" to maintain a house.[5] Denying the female side of science costs us the potential services of hundreds of thousands of talented women scientists and purges the existence of eccentric female inventors like Frances GABe from public mythology.

It is a wonder that science happens at all, when it is left to men to handle. As Sally Hacker has shown, the men who self-select for engineering (and, to a somewhat lesser degree, science) prefer working with predictable things to working with unpredictable people.[6] They value in themselves a standardized pattern of emotional responses—total reliability, cautious thought, obsessive work, self-discipline, and an inability to express anger—that some psychotherapists have described as an "engineering syndrome."[7] These characteristics not only operate against the development of socially and ecologically responsible technology, they also mitigate against the likelihood of truly innovative thinking. Whether they choose scientific and engineering careers actively or are funneled into them, people with this personality structure are not likely to question the value systems supported by their contributions, to rock the social boat, or to make genuine scientific breakthroughs. These are people who will modify the existing structure, not change its direction; the "improved" future they create is just like the past, only faster, bigger, better, more so.

The same process of deceptive myth-making that occurs with individual discoveries also occurs with the overall picture of scientific history absorbed by a trusting public. Although we learn a history of linear scientific progress, culminating in "the-truth-as-we-know-it," the actual path of scientific achievement is anything but linear. It may be true, as Newton said, that "If [he had] seen further than others, it [was] by standing upon the shoulders of giants." It is not true, however, that all the giants were looking in the same direction.

More than two decades ago, Thomas Kuhn, in *The Structure of Scientific Revolutions*, elucidated the difference between "normal" science, in which researchers progressively accumulate data to support or modestly modify a generally accepted hypothesis, and scientific revolutions, like those of Darwin and Einstein, that result in the creation of a totally new world view or "paradigm," completely at variance with previous, and no longer adequate, explanations of how the world works.[8]

History, of course, is not a neutral tool. Public suspicion that the current state of scientific knowledge only possibly, not necessarily, provides a more accurate understanding of the universe than was available before, might seriously undermine the pre-eminent status of science—and scientists—as an incontrovertible source of truth. Science might even fall as low as law or politics, subject to the same, untrustworthy workings of relativist ethics. Oh, my! Oh, my! Because general press attention would quickly debunk that favorite myth of "progress" (the myth of "better" discussed in the last chapter), vested technological and scientific interests are hardly anxious to have Thomas Kuhn's analysis spread across the morning news. The recognition that tomorrow is not "better," just "different" could shatter an entire economic system based on the consumption of goods, each product a progressive step "up" from the one that preceded it.

Father Time

Technological determinism, then, is a complex phenomenon that encompasses both the apparent inevitability of certain technologies and the apparent linearity of their historical development. In some cases, science actively colludes with questionable technological developments. The scientific method can be used to render the results of investigation neutral, objective and thorough, as in the case of researchers who ignore as irrelevant the massive job loss for migrant workers caused by mechanically harvestable square tomatoes. Since important theoretical questions (e.g. about the nature of the atom) may be solved simultaneously with invention (e.g. the atom bomb), the scientific method also provides "cover" for disturbing technological developments. Similarly, tricky experimental techniques (e.g. for genetic engineering) are practiced regardless of the potential for their later misuse, letting some very dangerous genies out of the bottle. Without the protective coloration of the scientific enterprise, the myth of technological determinism would be much more difficult to sustain.

"Pure" science (basic research) frequently escapes the scrutiny for bias that visits other human activities. We rarely look at why certain scientific questions are "chosen" for close examination, who funds research, or who might benefit down the line from having certain answers. There are, to be sure, multiple reasons—not all of them self-interest—behind a research project; often the individual scientist, hiding behind a curtain of nonideological naivety, is not aware of concurrent forces operating to make particular research topics, like Hollywood screen stars, more "bankable."[9] Noble and altruistic goals—from solving the human identity question "who am I" to ending the suffering of cancer—are fragrant contributors to the scientific stew; their rosemary-and-thyme scent may incidentally mask an odor of intent that is not so sweet.

As basic research shades into applied research and then into technology, its practitioners polish their halos of neutrality and objectivity to reduce public debate, dissent or demur. The goal, of course, is to limit discussion that might result in funding cuts, job loss or a reduction in prestige. Consequently, there are only a few clearly visible points along the timeline of any research program at which input into the decision-making process is feasible or effective. Although they both take place primarily within the corporation or the academy, scientific research and technological development are subject to different decision-making structures.

Unlike the wealthy gentlemen of the eighteenth century who gained admission to the Royal Society of London through their amateur efforts in astronomy or natural history, today's scientists operate in a thoroughly professionalized environment. It is exceedingly difficult to get published, and impossible to receive grants, without advanced degrees and collegial support as credentials of worth. The Scientific Establishment operates on a peer review basis that almost totally excludes outsiders from participating in decision-making. While this process is supposed to guarantee that decisions are made by informed parties, it also guarantees that those with vested interests in particular fields (very few of whom are women) control the filters of recognition and funding, not always for the greater public good—or even for the greater understanding of nature. For instance, German geologist Alfred Wegener, who originated the theories of plate tectonic and continental drift, was ostracized by the scientific community for his views from 1912 until his death in 1930; his theories are now the accepted explanation for the creation of the existing continents from the original single continent of Pangaea, and are crucial to today's understanding of volcanoes, earthquakes, and the formation of the earth's crust.[10]

The tightly-locked peer door also explains why women find it so difficult to gain admission to the inner sanctums of science (only forty-nine women have been elected to the 1,371-member National Academy of Sciences, the most prestigious of US scientific organizations). As Rosabeth Moss Kanter showed in *Men and Women of the Corporation*, the first requirement of "peerdom" is to look like, walk like, and talk like those who already have a key; women scientists don't.[11]

There are three loci of decision-making in science: the individual's decision about what research to pursue; acquisition of funds to carry on research; and recognition of one's work in professional journals. The first decision is deeply affected by values internalized during long years of scientific education and socialization; a student learns what questions are "important" in her or his field and what activities will be rewarded with funds, academic position, company promotion, or peer recognition. The second decision, awarding funds from the coffers of government, foundations, universities, or internal research and development (R&D) budgets, is typically a competitive, political process, in which the crucial elements are the structure of the decision-making process itself and the composition of peer or corporate review committees (that is, who gets on them and whom the applicant knows). Similar peer review committees make the third decision, whose work will be published, by soliciting comments about the quality and value of a submission from others in the field.[12]

At each point, the "old boy" network and the grapevine play prime roles; a senior scientist/mentor and plenty of good contacts are absolutely necessary to get published and receive research funds. Until the number of women within each scientific profession reaches a critical mass, these decision-making loci will be extremely difficult to influence.[13] Occasionally, a woman can succeed independently of the system, as did Rachel Carson, who warned about poisoning the earth, air, and water long before ecology became fashionable, but more often women are left behind. Besides encouraging more women to enter scientific careers and emphasizing the importance of female mentors, we need to open up the decision-making process by employing more women in grant-dispensing units of federal agencies and foundations, and by including women scientists on financial, publication, and academic review committees in more than a token fashion.

At first glance, it may seem easier to influence the path of technological decision-making than the scientific one. To begin with, some technology does incubate in basements, garages, and small businesses. Second, the process of development, even within large corporations, is somewhat haphazard, although still quite expensive. And third, the volatile market, which can be—and usually is—manipulated, substitutes for peer-reviewed publication in according recognition. Broadly speaking, technology offers women far more pressure points that are vulnerable to influence than does science, but it is difficult to discern those points in the chaos. Business decisions often appear to be made by default, or by committees whose responsibility is deliberately so diffuse that it is hard to know who is responsible for what decision. One problem remains the same, of course, in both science and technology: too few women are involved.

If the initial phase of technological development takes place in a private environment, the individual woman may have a great deal of choice about what she produces. (The entre-

131

preneurial or inventive woman, however, is handicapped by the triple burdens of simultaneously supporting herself, financing a project, and caring for a family.) In corporations, except for the few that support entrepreneurial enclaves, decisions about technological direction generally come from the top, but a politically astute individual can wield great influence in the early stages of a project over such matters as user-friendliness, physical appearance, and appropriate application.

Foundation and government grants account for only a small portion of the funding for technological development. Most funding is generated through private (bank) financing, through private or public contracts to produce the particular product desired by those who circulate Requests for Proposals (RFPs), or through capital acquired by public stock offerings or the profitable sale of other goods. The decision-making process of the market is influenced by the interplay of market research, advertising, promotion, and distribution channels.

Although there are many "windows of vulnerability," each one is open for only a short while. Technological design is at its most flexible at the very beginning of the process. Other "windows" open at the beginning of each phase or subphase of technological implementation—financing, production, packaging, marketing, advertising—but the further along in the process, the smaller the impact of a decision on the final form of the product. Once production has begun, the possibilities of changing the physical format of a technology or halting its implementation are almost nil. Retooling is extremely expensive; employees already on the payroll would lose their jobs; egos are on the line. Only gross malfunction or a recognition that a company would be open to lawsuits of bankrupting proportions will do. For example, internal memos from General Motors presented at a jury trial indicated that the company had been aware of serious brake defects in their 1980 model X-cars;[14] the company apparently decided to risk lawsuits for injury and negligence because paying settlements would be cheaper than re-tooling factories. (GM was held liable for more than $5 million in damages in the first of more than fifty suits awaiting settlement.[15])

Because technology is so integral to the social matrix, the

overall status of women in society plays a comparably larger role in allocating technological power than it does in allocating power in strictly scientific occupations. To generate new technological concepts and alter development at the design-and-review stage, the number of women with special technical skills needs to be increased dramatically, but women who move into decision-making positions in management, patent law, contract evaluation, finance, marketing, advertising and distribution can also have a noticeable effect. As in science, however, the twin brakes of socialization through education and promotion-by-imitation often militate against women using their positions to bring about change. For women to invent new technologies successfully, they must be free to express alternate values in design, thought and managerial processes, they must receive financial support within the corporate political structure or from financial institutions, and they must be able to promote their products effectively in the market. Any one of these conditions is fairly difficult to meet; more than one, extraordinarily so.

Uncle Sam: kilodeaths per megabuck

World War II permanently warped the straightforward buyer/seller relationship that had existed between the US government and arms dealers into its contemporary form,[16] which the late president Dwight D. Eisenhower first labeled the "military-industrial complex." Compared to the devious dealings that now pass for "business as usual" at the Pentagon, Andrew Undershaft, the mercenary arms manufacturer in George Bernard Shaw's *Major Barbara*, is innocence incarnate. Today's arms dealers derive their profits from a total lack of market competition: the cost-plus pricing, sole source contracts, and guaranteed sales proffered by the government encourage inefficient management, high overhead rates and excessive waste.[17]

Enormous amounts of government research money poured into the development of radar, sonar, computer technology and the atomic bomb during World War II, creating a defense industry so dependent on federal dollars that it could pass for

133

nationalized. Compared to consumer industries doing the same volume of business, defense contractors in 1983 used less than half the amount of shareholder-invested capital to finance their operations. The capital they risk belongs to taxpayers instead.[18] In theory, defense industries are subsidized because they must depend on only one market—the government—for sales. True, the politicized weapons procurement process can stop contracts cold, and true, the demand for state-of-the-art technology forces production into inefficient, expensive bursts of batch manufacturing. But the Pentagon's relatively risk-free bucks provide the biggest incentive for maintaining the status quo.[19]

In the United States, defense consumed $270 billion, or approximately 25 percent, of the 1983 fiscal year budget; of that number $24.5 billion was devoted specifically to military and aerospace R&D.[20] In the UK defense expenditure totaled almost £16 billion in 1983-4.[21] Even much of the private sector's R&D expenditures of roughly $34 billion in the same year was spent on defense-related research in electrical and communications equipment, aircraft, missiles, machinery and motor vehicles.[22] Rather than encouraging economic growth, bloated defense budgets generate an inflationary spiral, increase pressure for high interest rates, divert capital and scarce resources from consumer to defense technologies, and use human resources inefficiently.[23] Although defense spending does create jobs (more than 70 percent of which are male job slots[24]), studies show that "dollar for dollar more jobs are created through such public endeavors as construction, transit systems, health services, and schools."[25]

Commercial spin-offs from space and defense research are supposed to justify this defense-weighted ratio. The Army has given us food packaged in boilable retort pouches instead of metal cans, freeze-dried coffee, and left- and right-footed hiking boots; thanks to NASA's space program women have Tang, Teflon and a better refrigerator door, as well as a cordless, miniature vacuum-cleaner and a bra for jogging. However, money spent directly on commercial innovation might have produced these, or equivalent products, at a much lower cost in a much shorter time.

134

By comparison, in 1983 the US government allocated only $13.9 billion dollars for all other research and development activities, to be shared among such competing areas as health, energy, transportation, natural resources and education.[26] The nearly 2:1 ratio between government allocations for defense and nondefense R&D implies, correctly, that the greatest number of opportunities for doing research in the United States lies in military areas that are historically horrifying and hostile to most women. The "gender gap" between men's and women's support for President Reagan's defense spending shows clearly that more than 60 percent of all American women would prefer a different set of budget priorities.[27]

Such a pattern of allocations could not survive the budget process without the support of many people *outside* whichever administration is in power. In many cases, the very scientists and engineers who sport "neutrality" buttons on both lapels argue as hard for the inclusion of their own special interests as do Congressional representatives seeking a pork-barrel post office, dam or army base in their district. Professional organizations, such as the Institute of Electrical and Electronics Engineers, lobby actively to continue funding for projects that employ their members, from the Clinch River breeder reactor to permanent space stations to Star Wars laser weapons, whether or not the project will benefit society as a whole. These organizations of "experts," which are often called upon to give "objective" advice to both the executive and legislative branches of government, do not preach from a neutral pulpit. It is rare indeed for these groups, composed predominantly of white males, to support research that would address women's special needs, or even to acknowledge that a distinctly separate interest exists. (Many of these professional organizations do now have women's caucuses, but the women's agendas are often slighted by the larger organization.)

The weight of these professional special interest groups, combined with the interests of the bureaucracy and the smallest impetus to create a new technology (a feasibility study, perhaps), is enough to generate almost unstoppable momentum, even for thundering white elephants like the nuclear power industry. No conspiracy theory is needed to explain the process: the same way a snowball rolling downhill collects more and more snow, the longer a technology is thought about or produced in any form, the more it gathers adherents, proponents, investors, managers, users and institutional advocates, all of whom have a vested interest in recouping the time, money or influence they have spent. If R&D has been subsidized by the government, then the bureaucrat who "signed off" on the project will have the biggest stake in proving that the investment was wise; if a company invests its resources, then the project manager and executives who approved the investment will lead the charge.

The surface absurdity of this situation becomes more comprehensible if we forget all the nonsense we've been told about how the consumer demand drives technology. The driver for technological development is more than a need that must be fulfilled; it is more than the invention of a tool or process that makes a product possible; it is more even than powerful egos. Although each of these drivers plays a role in bringing a technology from concept to reality, the tallest driver behind the wheel of technology is money.

Take, for example, the growth of cable television. Cable is an inherently regressive technology. The cable itself is redundant; almost all homes are already wired for telephone services (although ordinary phone lines cannot accommodate visual images) when cable is installed. The technology is outdated; direct broadcast satellites that will increase channel capacity just as much as coaxial cable are already on the market; they were on the horizon even when the cable industry began its period of explosive growth, followed by merger and acquisition fever, in the mid-to-late 1970s. The need is limited; only those in rural areas and in some particularly crowded urban centers require another means of receiving a television signal clearly. Large companies got into cable not because of a need, not because of a new invention, but because some executive put his ego on the line; companies got into cable because they thought they saw a way of making money. They were wrong.[28]

Although cable TV now wires together about 50 percent of all television in the United States, companies are losing money from their investments. Time Inc., Westinghouse, Times-

Mirror Cablevision, Cox Cable, and Warner/Amex Cable, after buying up many small, independent cable companies and forming pay-TV programming services, now seek to divest themselves of their cable programming divisions; CBS Cable and the Entertainment Channel have already gone out of business.[29] Will this white elephant technology be abandoned, then, and supplanted by something more innovative? Not on your life. To position themselves for future profits, cable companies intend, like AT&T, to offer interactive videotex services as an alternative to television programs.[30] In some cases utility companies, which see cable as a money-saving means of automating meter-reading, billing and energy management, are buying into systems.[31] We're stuck with it.

Cable television offers a wry lesson on the persistence of a wrong-headed technology in spite of the market. This all-too-typical story points out several weaknesses in our system of technological management. Companies are using defective cost/benefit studies when they decide to make an investment; they are not correcting for vested interests, bandwagon effects or diseconomies of scale. (Small, decentralized businesses may spread out risk, maintain more efficient management, and provide better service.) Large corporations look over their shoulder and see someone else making money and say "me too." These assessment mechanisms have a serious flaw: they deal only with the cost/benefit ratio for the producer of the technology. The cost/benefit ratio for the ultimate user of a technology is often distorted to support what the study-makers perceive to be the desired conclusion. Buying into their own myth of objectivity, companies assume that the studies show the "truth."[32]

Such "truths" deceive us all—and we pay dearly for the deception.

[11]
Qui bono?

Before we can effectively alter the apparently inevitable course of a particular technology, we need to understand who benefits from it. Such a determination is rarely easy, particularly if we focus only on the long-term social implications of a product or method and ignore the individuals who have a stake in its success. Often, women's self-consciousness about their lack of technical expertise inhibits them from recognizing the pattern of short-term, personal gain that lies behind almost all large-scale technological innovations. But lack of technical knowledge need not prevent us from seeing beyond the myths of technological determinism and capitalistic cabals, or from taking action in our own interest.

The dismal history of cable television, with losers all around, should be enough to cast reasonable doubt on a conspiracy theory of technological development. A true "capitalist conspiracy" explanation of the cable fiasco would satisfy our desire for white hats and black hats with images of schemers plucking dollar signs out of "rabbit ear" antennas, while their victims grub for survival in a field full of old picture tubes. The reality is more accurately described as a merry-go-round, with individual horses rising and falling, while the wheel of technology turns and turns.

Only occasionally can we determine clearly who benefits from a particular technological innovation: farmers want to keep using the carcinogenic pesticide ethylene dibromide (EDB), instead of replacing it with a more expensive alternative or losing crops; manufacturers want to leave cake mixes with a minute portion of EDB on grocery store shelves, rather than recall and destroy their stocks. Consumers, who face either a short-term price increase or a long-term health risk, are the victims; winners and losers are clear. But in most circumstances, those ever-shifting merry-go-round horses make it terribly frustrating to identify the "enemy." Those who never get on the carousel are obviously out of the game, but not all those who manage to scramble into a saddle are winners.

Who's the winner and who's the loser, for instance, when a company offers "Recipe Chef" software that "addresses the often neglected homemaker"? The "experienced data processing professional" who wrote the program? The publisher who buys the software? The author of the "56-page illustrated User's Guide" for this "easy-to-use" program, which requires an IBM PC with 64K, an 80-column display card, and at least one disk drive (just the thing to put on the kitchen counter)?[1] The advertising agency that promotes the product? The package designer? Or everyone who buys recipe software that creates more work than it saves? At some point in the process everyone involved stands to lose or gain from the product.

In our divide-and-conquer system of political economics, people end up fighting with each other whenever a "villain" sets them off or whenever it becomes too difficult to figure out just who the "villain" is. Politically, this strategy operates to the benefit of the "villain," since everyone is too busy struggling against one another to make a concerted effort to bring about change. In this case, trying to figure out whether the software publisher, the programmer or the advertiser will make the most money distracts us from figuring out why women aren't using computers and why home computers have become a technological solution in search of a problem. Assuming that the person or company that gains the most from a given technology must have been the driving force behind it, we spend our time pointing fingers instead of making change.

Whether or not the "villain" is hiding deliberately, we are fighting the wrong battles with the wrong people. First, "snapshots" showing the relative positions of everyone's horse at different times in the technological cycle are the best we can expect to achieve. Second, although long-term consequences

Figure 11.1 Recipe software (*Virtual Combinatics*)

may be of the greatest social concern, it is the short-term gains and losses shown in each "snapshot" that depict the factors most important to the individuals involved in designing or implementing a technology. Will they be promoted? Will they make more money through wages or stock? Will they have more power or less? Will they receive credit for improving the bottom line on the company's quarterly report? Locating pressure points vulnerable to change means locating those individuals who will perceive *near-term* risks or benefits for themselves. In order to change a technology before it becomes too entrenched, we need to focus on the smaller, multiple culprits, and forget about the single, hard-to-find "villain."

Process versus product

Booming voices fill television screens, legislative halls, academic conferences, and even, occasionally, executive retreats with great debates about the long-term social impacts of new technology. Such debates, however, rarely take place where they might matter: at design reviews, in board rooms, or around a drafting table. Decisions about technology are not reached through a long process of public debate or even through a tough process of corporate give-and-take; they are generally reached on an *ad hoc* basis by individuals deciding what will benefit their companies and themselves, not society.

According to common argument, since no one really knows what's best for society and since there is no viable mechanism for consumer input until a product is on the shelves, we must just let the "free" market sort out the consequences. Market researchers assess consumer demand for new products and test them for modification and promotion, but they do not evaluate whether a product should be developed in the first place. More importantly, market research tests *response* to an item; it doesn't ask what people *want* or let them suggest alternatives. As we have seen, there is no "free" market in technology; the market process arrives too late to be free.

For instance, we will all pay for nuclear power plants whether or not they ever produce any electricity, whether or not we want—or even need—them. A decision made decades ago, with "the best of intentions," can haunt both ratepayers and stockholders with huge debts on costly, dangerous, incomplete power plants supposedly built to provide cheap electricity during an erroneously forecast shortage. Obviously, the "best of intentions" begs the cynical question of "best for whom?" Typically, stockholders made money off the nuclear industry in the short term. Certain utility company executives, government figures on the former US Atomic Energy Commission (now the Nuclear Regulatory Commission) and elected politicians gained tremendous power from the millions of construction dollars they controlled. During the building boom, other utility company employees, from purchasing agents to bookkeepers, from engineers to blue-collar workers, gained well-paid employment. But the stock- and bond-holders and company exectives now being held accountable for the nuclear power debacle in Washington state are rarely the same ones who benefited from the original decision to build the plants. (Many suggestible middle- and upper-income individuals lost their life savings when the Washington Power Supply System, derogatorily nicknamed "Whoops," defaulted on its loans in 1983). And different construction workers now bemoan the loss of jobs as nuclear power plant construction screeches to a halt.

To counteract the many narrowly focused constituencies of a technology, we must learn to find the equivalent, or even better, set of benefits that flow from an alternative technological choice. Negative campaigns rarely succeed against the temptation of immediate access to money, jobs and power. Had there been a countervailing force of people who would have benefited in the *short term* from solar power in the 1950s, for instance, the *long-term* results might have been much less expensive and destructive. In other words, a holier-than-thou attitude that threatens culprits with radioactive wastes will never be as convincing an argument as a specific opportunity to make more money geothermally.

The name of the game

Politics—the allocation of power and resources on either a corporate or public level—thus channels technology into those specific areas of growth that are of most immediate benefit to those who master the process. To have a successful impact on a discriminatory technological economy, women must break out of the political ghetto of public and social service issues. Equal education, reproductive rights, welfare, health care, day care, and wife abuse are areas of critical concern to women, but action in these areas will not sufficiently protect women's interests in the future.

When former President Jimmy Carter fired Bella Abzug from her position as co-chair of his Women's Advisory Committee in 1978, he explicitly denounced her claim that the economy is a woman's issue.[2] The consequence of Abzug's heretical insistence on playing in the big boys' sandbox indicates the powerful importance men attach to their control over the economy. But when two out of three of all adults living in poverty in the US are women,[3] when female senior citizens are deprived of subsistence because adquate pensions and social security payments are tied to long periods of consecutive employment,[4] when women work without pay in the home, when they are denied equal employment opportunities in an expanding, but gender-segregated technological workforce, when women in the US in 1982 earned only 62 cents for every male dollar,[5] and in the UK less than 64p for every male pound, there is no question that Abzug was right.

Whenever women are muscled out of decision-making in any area, including defense, we must immediately suspect that our interests are being sacrificed. How do women benefit from massive defense budgets, for example? If spending on transportation or environmental protection would generate more jobs, a higher percentage of which would be open to women, and would better catalyze the economy, why do defense industries continue to receive so much funding? It is no accident that women have moved to the forefront of the peace movement: Randall Forsberg, founder of the Nuclear Freeze campaign, Petra Kelly, parliamentary representative of the Green Party in West Germany, the women of Greenham Common and the Women's Peace Encampment in Romulus, New York, have all made peace a woman's issue. They have been less successful, however, in putting women's concerns onto an agenda that the peace movement must address.

Until we acknowledge just how much large, male-dominated corporations, banks and labor unions benefit in the *short term* from defense spending and learn to ignore the rhetoric of national security as a distraction from the *real* issues of personal gain, we will not succeed in defining equally tempting alternatives, independent of the rhetoric of peace. Peace will not be possible until it becomes profitable—and, paradoxically, more expensive.[6] (Perhaps we should offer subsidies to defense contractors not to make bombs, the same way we offer subsidies to farmers not to grow grain.)

The limited time available for generating a dramatic shift in defense or any other technological investment grows shorter almost daily. Economically brittle, post-industrial societies do not expand; they merely oscillate between recession and inflation. Since economic growth is no longer reliable as a social equalizer (the middle class cannot continue to expand unless income is redistributed), the culture has become increasingly class-conscious. Fear of losing their pre-eminent status paralyzes individual policy-makers into quickly selecting the most traditional of alternatives in a form of protective reaction. This desire to "cover their own ass" first weights the wheel of change in their favor. An example may make this clear.

Creeping corporatism

Over the last few years, the burgeoning personal computer industry has changed from a decentralized and highly individualized activity, taking place in living rooms, basements, garages and numerous small companies, to a massive, expensive effort centralized in several dozen corporate headquarters.[7] Business theorists rationalize this process as the unusually rapid but natural growth of an industry from an entrepreneurially driven hobby into a mature, marketing-driven enterprise. Such theorists see, quite accurately, that large production, distribution, advertising and marketing organizations are in the best position to raise the capital needed to thoroughly exploit the market.

Business theorists, however, ignore the role played in this

"natural" process by protective reaction, which ensures that corporations "take cover" against the risk of innovation by taking control of the technology. Corporatism has quickly degraded the central but unpredictable role of media-hyped, instantly rich individual programmers into the traditional corporate "me too" ethic: "more of the same is better." (IBM waited for new companies like Apple to establish a demand for small computers and then moved in six years later to take a one-third market share; large publishing companies are bounding into the software market for fear of losing out in the competition for the consumer dollar; large entertainment conglomerates moved into videogames in hopes of making a quick buck, as Warner Brothers planned to do when it acquired the now-floundering Atari.) As a result, more and more videogames look alike, business software products imitate each other, and the rate of computer innovation spirals downward (British computer maverick Clive Sinclair notwithstanding).

In terms of implications for creating a technology to meet women's needs, "protective reaction" mandates two strategic tactics. First, women must be involved in setting the terms of new technologies during the initial "incubator" stages of development. Women were not sufficiently involved in defining the parameters of computer technology and software; now, even when employed by major companies, they must struggle with the corporate albatross to make changes after the fact. Second, women must confront large corporations in the marketplace, the only place that matters. As long as companies continue to make money by repeating the past, there is no reason for them to do otherwise. The same women who boycotted beef when prices got too high have the power to boycott recipe software that would waste their time typing recipes for stroganoff, stew and boeuf bourguignon.

From sow's ear to silk purse

For a variety of reasons, women's political organizations seem to find it more difficult to confront technology than to combat legal discrimination. These groups are so busy trying to deal with the very real and immediate demands of the present that they put the future on hold. Women's groups must address a complex, contemporaneous agenda to seek political and economic equity. Everything from nonsexist textbooks to contraceptives is on the list; setting priorities among such varied and compelling issues seems almost impossible. The consequent fragmentation of attention and funds can drain an organization, leaving it unable to cope effectively with any one of its concerns. The mere thought of adding technology as another item can be overwhelming.

Additionally, many of the women who are now politically active are themselves victims of math anxiety and computer phobia. Their own fear, insecurity or lack of knowledge about science and technology makes them understandably reluctant to take up the cudgels of change. Unfortunately, we don't have the luxury of waiting for our less-fearful daughters to grow up. If we don't take action, especially to guarantee that technophobia doesn't turn out to be a hereditary condition, another whole set of change-resistant technologies may be in place.

Women's lack of capital also makes it extremely difficult for them to compete in the capital-intensive environment of technology. Long-standing economic discrimination means that women are standing several rungs down the ladder; continually focusing women's attention on consumer aspects of the economy leaves many women unfamiliar with financing anything more than a car.

These liabilities can be turned into assets. We do have the political skill and experience to attack technological development. We do know how to determine who benefits in the short-term from a particular technology. We do know how to find vulnerable pressure points to bring about change. And we are certainly capable of applying our common sense and intuition to technological problems in order to define our own solutions.

PART III

Tomorrow is a Woman's Issue

[12]
Taking charge of tomorrow

The questions gnaw at us, nibble away at our confidence, no matter how much we understand about the process of technological development. Why aren't more women involved? Why has progess been so slow? Why is change so difficult? True, the patterns of male domination of technology have been burnished by time to a high patina. But the size and historical roots of the technological problem don't provide an adequate explanation for the lack of attention it has received; not when women have attacked so many equally recalcitrant social issues. Having earlier made the argument that control over the man-made, material world is a necessary, albeit not sufficient, condition for women to gain control over their own lives, it is time to explore institutional difficulties beyond those of design and production, and specify strategies for dealing with all phases of the technological process.

Pessimism of the mind

It is impossible to underestimate the enormity of the situation we confront. Technology is intimately intertwined with economic development and, in Western society, with capitalism. Since changing the characteristics of this entire system of political economics is unlikely, certainly within our lifetimes, we must break off vulnerable bits of it. Technology has a real, material form; we cannot change it in our heads; we must change it in the real, material, *commercial* context in which it exists.

149

Thus, we must confront the unpleasant fact that Emerson was wrong. Buiding a better mousetrap is not enough for the world to beat a path to one's door. In the real, contemporary, mass-marketed world, we must inform people that a better mousetrap exists, convince them that they want to buy the improved version, and provide a convenient means of purchase. In other words, advertising, marketing and distribution are just as important, if not more so, than inventing an enticement superior to cheese. Until we see ourselves as producers, not just consumers, of technology, we will continue to perceive such techniques as unfair means of manipulating the market. Instead of recoiling with horror, or resisting advertising appeals with a shrug of the intellectual's shoulder, women need to examine why advertising and marketing techniques are so effective and decide which ones to adapt to their own purposes.

Taking direct action is much more effective than boycotting bad products which, while sometimes a useful tactic, remains a reactive, after-the-fact response to an unsafe or outrageous technology. Boycotting succeeds only when it threatens a significant loss of sales; it means nothing if the boycotters don't represent those who would otherwise buy a technology. The farmworkers' lettuce and grape boycotts of the 1960s and 1970s were successful because many people participated, because there were other brands of produce that could be purchased for the same price, and because the items were not essential. When Women Against Pornography and other groups decided to protest against the sexist videogame "Custer's Revenge" (see page 117), they realized that a boycott would be meaningless, since their numbers were small and didn't represent potential buyers anyway. Instead, they developed an effective media campaign, using the very same publicity tools used by American Multiple Industries, the manufacturer of the game, but exploiting the media for a very different goal.

Compared to the problems of getting good products onto the market, getting the bad ones off is easy. Even if it has good advertising and marketing, a wonderful product may be ignored or destroyed before consumers have a chance to see it because of the difficulty of moving a new product from a manufacturer to wholesalers and then to dealers. At every step along the way, buyers at other levels must be "sold" on the product, and on its packaging, before it can appear on the shelves. As consumers, we tend to think of sales people only in terms of their persuasive relationship to the ultimate purchaser, not in terms of their other role as intermediate buyers who need to be convinced about the worth and profitability of a product.

These middlemen, who are often more conservative than the general public, buy in large volume. Since they take a much larger financial risk than a final purchaser, they are wary about new technology that is not well-supported by advertising, that conflicts with their own expectations, or that differs from other products. Because of their reluctance to try something new and different, wholesalers and dealers form a narrow channel through which technology must pass from the bay of producers to the ocean of consumers.

One other word of warning about the real world: the easiest way to make money in this economy is to steal it. Never mind robbing banks or ripping off cheap copies in Hong Kong. Stealing in this context refers to companies that imitate a successful product, especially one produced by a small business lacking the financial, production, legal and marketing muscle of its larger competitors. The inventor or entrepreneur must invest money, time and effort in research and development that the copycat company doesn't need to expend. Companies of all sizes are also known to practice such Faginesque exercises as industrial spying, pocketing proprietary material under discussion, and buying up patents to *prevent* a superior, competing product from reaching the market.

The bottom line, is, unfortunately, the bottom line. Technology costs money—lots of it. The "poor nerd-to-millionaire nerd" fantasy of the popular press describes only a minute fraction of people who have a great product to sell.[1] Being lucky, being in the right place at the right time, having the right contacts, and wearing pants instead of skirts all play a role in developing and marketing a new technology; but none is as important as money. Research and design costs money: if you do it yourself, you must have savings to live on, another job to pay the bills, inherited wealth, or a hefty line of credit. Production and packaging cost money. Advertising and promotion cost money. Money costs money (interest). Creating ways to finance technological women must therefore be part of our strategy to make way for women in technology.

Five rules to risk by

These rules may appear excessively cynical, but they realistically describe what happens when women try to turn dreams of technological change into reality:

1 Women who follow all the rules are being had; the first rule is that there are no rules. We must forget *everything* we've been told about being assertive, being team-players, or dressing for success. The people who formulate those rules don't have our best interests in mind.
2 When Bambi meets Godzilla, Godzilla wins. Technology is a risky business that affords no time for fairy tales. A healthy respect for the opposition will keep us from underestimating just how long it may take and how hard we will have to work to make our dreams come true.
3 We must never allow others to determine our value by what we're paid or how we're treated. As Eleanor Roosevelt said, "No one can make [us] feel inferior without [our] consent." Many of those who are busy "looking out for Number One" do so by making us Number Two.
4 We need to spend a buck to make a buck. The stock market, or even the race track, is probably safer than new technology as a sink for our funds so we must think carefully about the risk involved.
5 There's a common saying in the women's movement: "Whatever women do, they must do twice as well as men to be thought of as half as good."[2] The phrase still holds true in technology, but the numbers are something like sixteen times as good to get one-sixteenth as far. This may not be difficult, but it's damn frustrating.

Rated X for anger

If the problems of altering the course of technology didn't seem insurmountable before, they probably do now. The long, complicated process of technological development demands highly educated, technically knowledgeable insiders to stop bad design in its tracks, or technically knowledgeable innovators with the time and financial resources to design new products independently. Influencing government and corporate programs for the assessment and evaluation of technology requires intimate familiarity with both the procedures and the personnel involved. Large amounts of capital, sophisticated marketing techniques, and access to an extensive distribution mechanism are prerequisites to successfully disseminating a new technology.

Given these realities, change seems as impossible as the situation seems intolerable. The blood boils at the unfairness of it all! But there is no time for despair. Nor do we have the luxury of being afraid of the future. The only solution is to turn our fear into anger and our anger into action. The blueprint follows: Read on.

Optimism of the will

The most important factor in making change is choosing a realistic goal. Success will breed new challenges and the confidence to take them on; picking a fight that can't be won will only breed discouragement. The first step is to break down the problem to one part of one technology. Select something you feel passionate about, whether it's training women to become systems analysts or electronic technicians, developing mass transit alternatives that meet women's needs, creating high-tech cottage industries that are safe and well-paid, reducing the rate of Caesarean sections at local hospitals, generating a feminist database, controlling recombinant DNA research, eliminating the hazardous and stressful consequences of video display terminals and office automation, converting arms manufacturing facilities into more benign uses, preventing the invasion of privacy by telecommunications technology, replacing nuclear power with decentralized photovoltaic cells, controlling toxic and radioactive waste disposal, eliminating sexist imagery in videogames and technical advertising and at industrial tradeshows, or building a truly useful home robot. The list is endless, the passion critical. You will need to touch that passion—and your anger—whenever things get rough. And things will get rough!

After you've spent some time at the library to research the issue, the second step is to form alliances and allegiances with other groups that already share your concern: technology doesn't usually reach the market based on the efforts of one person working alone in a basement, so change can't be brought about that way either. Research *all* potential collaborators, regardless of what you think of their other agendas. Politics makes strange bedsisters; it's one of the most enjoyable parts of the game. Some of the most traditional organizations, like the YWCA, the Girl Scouts or the American Association of University Women may just surprise you with their far-sighted leadership. These organizations have an extensive network of contacts among local and national political leaders, employ effective lobbyists, can mobilize large numbers of people and are experienced at raising funds.

Caucuses of women in professional organizations represent another useful resource: they have their own, often congruent, agendas for personal advancement, they have the essential technical knowledge and vocabulary to serve as informed advocates on technical issues, and they definitely know the most intimate ropes—and vulnerable spots—of the corporations involved in the technology you are examining. Also, consider local academic departments as a source of energy and information: friendly faculty members make excellent backers, provide expert knowledge, and often have students who will work for credit as unpaid interns on your project. Don't forget local politicians, whether or not they represent your district, and women who are politically active. They are a tremendous source of information about existing government activity, they have excellent networks of influential contacts, and those who support your cause are often willing to carry legislation that you research and propose.

Figure 12.1 Ms. Pacman (*Atari, Inc.*)

HAPPY VALENTINE'S DAY FROM ATARI

"I'm more than Pac-Man with a bow."

Wouldn't you love to find a Valentine with a real appetite for fun and games?

Then come to my exciting new house from Atari. It's just like my home in the arcade.

With four a-mazing floor plans. Four different exit patterns. And a dazzling variety of color schemes to go with them.

There's always plenty to eat, too. Apples, oranges, pears, bananas, even pretzels floating all over the place.

So whatatya say, stranger? I'm the only one like me. MS.PAC-MAN. And I'm only from Atari.

Certainly the women's movement, in all its shapes and guises, can offer enormous assistance in articulating women's needs and pressing for change. Whether or not a movement organization can stretch its resources to cover the future, when it's already spread thinly over a dozen different fronts in the present, must be evaluated on a case-by-case basis. Don't ask a group for resources that it can't possibly supply. At a time of economic hardship, when women must focus their efforts on personal economic survival, it is difficult for these organizations to acquire the necessary influx of additional people and money to attack new issues. While many of these groups recognize the futility of winning today's battle only to lose tomorrow's war, their day-to-day struggles frequently take precedence over long-range strategy. Some women in these groups, opposed to technology altogether out of either ignorance or of historically earned disgust, are adamant about seeking social change without it. Although these groups may not be able to offer financial support, personnel or knowledgeable professionals in your area, they often have other unmatched resources: mailing lists, press contacts and media experience.

Other organizations committed to social change abound, dealing with consumer, anti-nuclear, ecological, economic reform and civil rights issues. Their agendas may superficially parallel women's concerns about energy use, health hazards caused by nuclear and chemical wastes, or dangerous products, but be cautious. Although these groups may be more than willing to use female-supplied energy and money, some of them have not been so quick to offer reciprocal support for women's concerns. See if women hold positions of leadership in these organizations, or if they are just making coffee and running the copying machines; an organization in which women's voices go unheard and their concerns unheeded will prove to be a frigid partner.

Even among various cause-oriented groups, there is no consensus about technology. Labor organizations are vocal proponents of nuclear power and lower clean air standards as a way of creating jobs; Black organizations favor less environmental regulation of energy development for the same reason; ecologists savor environmental purity over develop-

156

ment—or women's convenience. While on the whole, such groups may provide additional weight on the lever of change, women cannot rely on them to act consistently on women's behalf. "We were urged to weigh our lives against the lives of our children. Our survival against the beauty of this place. . . . We never chose ourselves," reminds Susan Griffin.[3] Creating a future for women is something we must do on our own.

Women are frequently in the forefront of one movement that is often overlooked. Neighborhood organizations, block clubs and tenant groups, all of which constantly confront local power structures, are sometimes dismissed as "unimportant" by men. This leaves a power vacuum, allowing women to occupy vacant niches and emerge as leaders. (That's how New York City councilors Ruth Messinger and Carol Bellamy and Representative Barbara Mikulski (D-MD) got their start.) As these groups increase their sophistication and power, they move from stop signs and street lights to energy and the economy, attacking utility company rate structures and local corporate employment practices. If their political energy can be hitched to a technological issue with a strong local component, the potential for changing technological policy is immediately enhanced. Why? Because these groups know how to turn out voters, organize demonstrations, and embarrass elected and corporate officials alike into taking positive action. Given the added plus of their experienced, dynamic female leadership, a coalition with neighborhood organizations might provide an interesting and effective mechanism for changing the course of technological development.

Lasting change also requires a commitment to change the educational process that separates ethics from science and science from women. Neither change is easily achieved. Incorporating science and technology into liberal arts and women's studies curricula and women's values into technical studies ultimately demands a change in the way we divide knowledge. There are, however, some interim strategies for gaining a foothold. Since getting technology into a female-controlled area of study is easier than getting new values into a male-controlled field, one approach is to incorporate technology into women's studies curricula, before infiltrating scientific and engineering disciplines with women who have a

GONNA BE AN ENGINEER

© CONSTRUCTED by PEGGY SEEGER

EASILY

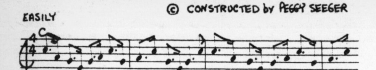

When I was a lit-tle girl I wished I was a boy, I tagged a-long be-hind the gang & wore my

cor-du-roys, Every-body said I on-ly did it to an-noy, But I was gon-na be an en-gi-neer.

MOM-MA TOLD ME "CAN'T YOU BE A LA-DY? YOUR DU-TY IS TO MAKE ME THE MOTH-ER OF A PEARL

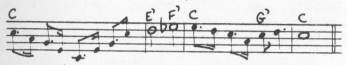

WAIT UN-TIL YOU'RE OLD-ER, DEAR, AND MAY-BE YOU'LL BE GLAD THAT YOU'RE A GIRL."

(this part only after verses 1, 3, 6 & 7)

DAIN-TY AS A DRES-DEN STA-TUE, GEN-TLE AS A JER-SEY COW, SMOOTH AS SILK,

gives creamy milk: LEARN TO COO, LEARN TO MOO, That's what to do to be a lad-y now.

NOTE: the words take some fitting into the above skeletal tune - but if not sung too fast the song sings well.

Taking charge of tomorrow

When I was a little girl, I wished I was a boy.
I tagged along behind the gang and wore my corduroys.
Everybody said I only did it to annoy,
But I was gonna be an engineer.

   Momma told me, "Can't you be a lady?
   Your duty is to make me the mother of a pearl
   Wait until you're older dear, and maybe,
   You'll be glad that you're a girl."

     Dainty as a Dresden statue,
     Gentle as a Jersey cow,
     Smooth as silk, gives creamy milk,
     Learn to coo, learn to moo,
     That's what to do to be a lady now.

When I went to school I learned to write and how to read,
Some history, geography, and home economy.
And typing is a skill that every girl is sure to need
To while away the extra time until the time to breed.
And then they had the nerve to say, "What would you like to be?"
I says, "I'm gonna be an engineer."

   No, you only have to learn to be a lady,
   And the duty isn't yours to try and run the world.
   An engineer could never have a baby.
   Remember, dear, that you're a girl.

So I became a typist and I study on the sly,
Working out the day and night so I can qualify.
Every time the boss comes in he pinched me on the thigh,
Says, "I've never had an engineer."

   Oh, you owe it to the job to be a lady.
   It's the duty of the staff to give the boss a whirl.
   The wages that you get are crummy, maybe,
   But it's all you get 'cause you're a girl.

     She's smart for a woman;
     I wonder how she got that way . . .
     You got no choice, you got no voice
     Just stay mum, pretend you're dumb.
     That's how you come to be a lady today.

Then Jimmy come along and we set up a conjugation.
We were busy every night with lovin' recreation.
Spent my days at work so he could get his education.
Now, he's an engineer.

He says, "I know you'll always be a lady.
It's the duty of my darling to love me all my life.
Could an engineer look after or obey me?
Remember, dear, that you're my wife."

Well, every time I turn around there's something else to do.
Cook a meal, scrub a floor or wash a sock or two.
I listen in to Jimmy Young; it makes me want to spew.
I was gonna be an engineer!

Oh, I only wish that I could be a lady.
I could do the lovely things that a lady's supposed to do.
I wouldn't even mind if they would pay me.
Then I could be a person, too.

What price for a woman?
You can buy her for a ring of gold.
To love and obey without any pay;
You get your cook and your nurse, for better or worse.
You don't need a purse when a lady is sold.

But now the times are harder and my Jimmy's got the sack.
I went down to Vickers; they were glad to have me back.
But I'm a third class citizen; my wages tell me that.
But I'm a first class engineer.

The boss he says, "I'll pay you as a lady.
Well, you only got the job 'cause I can't afford a man.
With you I keep the profits high as may be,
You're just a cheaper pair of hands."

You've got one fault: you're a woman.
You're not worth the equal pay.
A bitch or a tart, you're nothing but heart.
Shallow and vain, ya' got no brain.
You even go down the drain like a lady today."

Well, I listened to my mother and I joined a typing pool.
I listened to my lover and I put him through his school.
If I listen to the boss, I'm just a bloody fool.
And an underpaid engineer.

I been a sucker ever since I was a baby.
As a daughter and a wife, a lover and a dear.
But I'll fight 'em as a woman, not a lady.
Yes, I'll fight 'em as an engineer.

Figure 12.2 "Gonna Be An Engineer" (*Words and music, Peggy Seeger, copyright Stormking Music, New York; available on Folkways Records, no. 8561*)

commitment to a feminist value system.

Of all the many reasons that women might avoid math and science careers, one must certainly be that young women don't want to work with "nerds," they don't want to be labeled "nerds," and they definitely don't want to be "nerds" when they grow up. Who can blame them? It's a most unappealing prospect. One British study intimated that stereotyped images of science and scientists are even more potent than negative peer or parental pressure in discouraging women from technical careers.[4] That media image is inaccurate, of course, conveying neither the personal gratification nor the social interaction that is as much a part of science or technology as of any other human activity.

The cure is many-fold. First, guarantee, by whatever means, that young women are exposed to plenty of female role models who embody the ability to combine intellectual curiosity with human feeling. Second, ensure that there is a critical mass of women in a course, instead of isolating them as token females in every lab class. Third, provide supportive, all-female environments for learning math, science and technical skills. For many years, the greatest number of women graduating with degrees in the hard sciences has come from women's colleges, where women are expected to perform successfully in every field. Several other networks exist to provide such environments: the EQUALS program at the Lawrence Hall of Science at the University of California at Berkeley, the Math/Science Network at Mills College in Oakland, California, the Women's Technical Institute in Boston, the Girls Into Science and Technology and Women Into Science and Engineering programs sponsored by the Equal Opportunities Commission in Great Britain.[5]

If such an opportunity doesn't exist in your community, create one. Insist that a local computer camp offer special sessions for women and girls (ComputerTown! USA in Menlo Park, California, did so with great success). Ask women in technical professions to offer enrichment classes for female students at all levels. Encourage the local women's resource center, the YWCA, or women's studies programs to sponsor classes in science and technology within their own environments. The inherent positive expectations of such programs will help women develop the necessary confidence to continue in a less friendly (and occasionally downright hostile) department or career.

On most campuses, science and engineering programs are so distant physically from women's studies that women in one program know nothing of the other's existence. Since it's not realistic to expect engineering students to seek out women's studies, the latter must take the responsibility of reconnoitering, recruiting and informing female students. You may find a bulletin board display of "Famous Men in Mathematics" (no women at all) in desperate need of correction, sympathetic department secretaries who will become allies, female faculty willing to teach a technical or scientific course through women's studies.

On a personal level, enroll your daughter and yourself in a computer course and make sure she continues to take math and science courses all the way through school. Like playing the piano, science and math are best learned while young;

Figure 12.3 Sidewalk software stand (*Hampton Publishing,* CES Daily News)

taking them up again in middle or golden age is easier if there is a base of dormant knowledge to be tapped.

If you are already a student or a professional in a technical field, make an "each one, teach one" commitment to share your hard-won technical knowledge with another woman—if not a daughter, a mother, if not a niece, a neighbor, if not a friend, a stranger. Those in the field also owe women, of this and succeeding generations, a commitment to change the nature of science and engineering education. If you are in science and engineering courses, start questioning the values behind what you're being taught (this isn't easy when you have a problem set due every week, but it's essential). If you're teaching such a course, include discussions about the moral and value questions that form a context for research and development. Insist that undergraduate curriculum requirements be amended to include courses in the history and ethics of science. Considering that most technical knowledge becomes outdated within five to ten years (and some within a mere 18 months), it makes more sense to incorporate a course in ethics that deals with eternally recurring questions than yet another major requirement.

Some creative strategies

We've already discussed how to create change within the existing structure, how to modify it, distract it, disturb it and distress it. These actions need not always be major, highly visible ones; a very small shift in direction can generate a very large change in result. In fact, some of the most effective techniques for social change come from taking small, but unexpected steps, from "drawing a bigger circle." By enlarging the dimensions of a given situation, calling on unusual allies, adopting an absolutely innovative approach, or applying a technique in an unanticipated way, we can completely befuddle the opposition and reach our goals before anyone figures out what has happened. In that spirit, the following strategies may start some wheels turning.

1 *Write one letter, send one dollar.* Generally speaking, technological issues are not the type for mass demonstrations.

They lack media appeal because they are complicated; they lack mass appeal because they are abstract and long-term. Just because traditional organizing tools are so rarely used, they can produce an enormous effect with relatively small numbers. It might take 500,000 letters or 200,000 demonstrators to convince a politician to support the Equal Rights Amendment, but 500 letters or twenty protestors complaining about Sweetheart robots or scantily clad women advertising new bombs[6] can bring out the press and bring about change. Technological development costs money, but it doesn't need to be raised with $10,000 contributions to a limited partnership. If every woman who hates housework would send Frances GABe $1, her self-cleaning house would be finished, she could patent her inventions, and all our lives would be a little easier.[7]

2 *Neighborhood production cooperatives*. Appalachian and Nova Scotian women form them to make quilts. Artists form them to rent studios and showcase their work. Dairy farmers form them to sell milk. Vegetarians form them to sell health foods. There is absolutely no reason women can't form cooperatives to program software, assemble electronics, provide local bus services, decentralize alternative energy sources, or invent new household technologies. Such cooperatives would distribute risk and investment over a larger number of people, ensure that health and safety requirements are met, reduce the possibility of sweatshop-style exploitation, offer the day care and flexible work schedules women need, and simultaneously fill the need for geographically based support networks.

3 *Financing feminism*. Socially responsible mutual and money market investment funds (Dreyfus Third Century Fund, Pax World Fund, Working Assets, Calvert Social Investment Fund, New Alternative Fund) have been set up to advise investors wishing to buy stock only in politically acceptable firms: no nuclear power or weapons companies, for instance, or no companies doing business with South Africa.[8] Now that more women are moving into professional occupations and have some money to invest, why not create an investment fund for women-owned and -operated, high-technology firms?

4 *A profitable venture.* It's high time to put women's money to work in a venture capital company that provides start-up funding, legal and patent assistance, and management support to women-owned firms concentrating on technological development. This doesn't mean organizations like American Woman's Economic Development Corporation, which offers assistance (but no capital) to women entrepreneurs entering primarily traditional fields, but a fund for women that could compete with Nolan Bushnell's Catalyst Technology venture capital company. Like other venture capital firms, this one would own a part of the entrepreneurial companies it finances, but most of the profits it makes would be reinvested in other new, high-technology projects that promise benefits to women.

5 *Progress out of profits.* Since capitalists are known for their willingness to sell the rope by which they will be hanged, defining—and delivering—a distinct women's market offers some potential for encouraging the development of particular technologies that meet women's needs. Explicitly acknowledging women's role in consumption activities, a feminist eqivalent to *Consumer Reports* or *Underwriters' Laboratory* could assess technologies for their harm, benefit, value or insignificance to women and publish their evaluations regularly through the broad, existing network of women's media, from traditional women's magazines to radical feminist quarterlies. Such an organized alternative might have warned women about superabsorbent tampons, which have been implicated in causing toxic shock syndrome, for instance. It could also solicit opinions about the technologies women *want* to have, and establish a buying club, discount service or mail order business that would market highly recommended technological items directly to women.

Righting out the anger

We've looked at some of the negative, fearful reasons that women need to be involved in technological change: to put an end to continuing efforts to devalue our contributions and de-skill our labor; to put an end to practices that are harmful to our health and well-being; to put an end to alienating and destructive technologies that threaten human survival. There are other, equally essential, positive reasons—beyond the fact that society can no longer afford to waste the intelligence and skills of half the human race—that compel women's full participation in the technological enterprise.

First, involvement with technology empowers women and engenders self-confidence. Learning how to manipulate the man-made environment (not the natural one, which demands respect, rather than exploitation), helps end the paralyzing sense of passivity, helplessness and dependency that can keep women from achieving the full control they seek over their own lives. Ironically, public participation in technology brings us back to the individual: women's progress is helical. If our personal victimization from technology has political roots, so, too, does the political change of the technological process become a matter of personal growth.

Second, instead of looking toward male values as ones to emulate, current feminist thinking reaffirms the worth and importance of a female approach to relationships, art, discourse and invention.[9] Revaluing the female would make a big difference in technology as well. It would reaffirm the importance of the ordinary and the day-to-day, as opposed to the current preoccupation with the singular and the monumental. (If more people worried about washing the dishes than about launching the missiles, perhaps we might have escaped the arms race.) Because it implies evaluating technology in terms of its impact on relationships with others, revaluing the female would encourage acceptance of the idea that technologies need not be developed just because they are possible; it would realign research priorities to emphasize improving the real lives of real people now.

Third, the practical, common-sense approach to problem-solving, which women have adopted from necessity and circumstance, actually represents the qualities that are most "human" and least replicable in a computer. Re-establishing a sense of worth for the human race may just turn out to require women's capacity for common-sense thinking.

These issues are not important just for women; they are important for everyone. Our society has assigned to women precisely those distinctive human characteristics missing from the public arena: compassion, interconnection with others, the desire to transmit cultural values, and a willingness to make sacrifices to secure a better future for the next generation. Women's contribution to technological development is essential to bring those characteristics back into the public sphere.

[13]

A different future altogether

It is tempting, but impractical, to imagine what the world would be like if women had been able to maintain their critical and extensive participation in technological innovation from prehistorical human society to the present day. It is, however, reasonable to consider how technology might evolve in the next twenty years if women become actively committed to directing current and foreseeable technologies to different ends. If we implement the strategies discussed in the preceding chapters, the following agenda could realistically be achieved by the year 2000. Unlike some futurists' agendas, this one doesn't try to predict the unpredictable, invent a personal utopia or forecast inventions for which no research has been done. The goals described below might provide, though, some gentle nudges towards a technology of liberation.

Private lives, public choices

Reproduction and privacy are the two rights most threatened by new technology. New technologies in those areas, as presently envisioned, allow certain people to exercise their "right" to have a child or use a credit card only at the price of yielding control over and information about their lives to someone else. There is no *technological* reason that such situations must exist: their persistence and structure have a political cause and a political purpose.

Understandably, single and/or infertile women who are desperately anxious to conceive a child consider *in vitro*

168

fertilization (IVF), embryo transfer, surrogate mother programs or artificial insemination to be answers to their deepest desire. Such programs remain under the control of predominantly male medical practitioners and are accessible only to those wealthy enough to afford an expensive, uninsured alternative to conceiving and bearing a child naturally. (As recently as February 1984 Blue Shield of California, one of the largest private medical insurance carriers in the United States, declined to reclassify IVF from an uncovered, experimental procedure to an insured one because of its ethical concerns about couples' marital status and the disposal of unused eggs removed from the female.[1])

If such procedures exist, it is patently unfair to make them available, whether by law or by practice, only to certain races or classes of women; an infertile woman should have the same right to bear a child as a fertile woman, who is not subject to scrutiny as a suitable candidate for parenthood. On the other hand, women who are willing to donate an egg or embryo or to be surrogate mothers also need protection from exploitation and possible injury. In every case, many more women need to be more involved in making decisions about reproductive technologies, their accessibility, availability, risks and profound consequences for everyone involved, including the future child. If abortion is a woman's private decision, should embryo transfer be also? Should counseling be required? Were women's interests adequately represented in the Blue Shield case above? Interestingly enough, abortion is the topic of vociferous debate, but comparatively little is said about reproductive engineering.

Following the lead of the Feminist Women's Health Center in Oakland, California, other women's clinics should establish sperm banks for artificial insemination, and consider becoming involved in programs for surrogate mothers or IVF. US organizations like NARAL (National Abortion Rights Action League), the Boston Women's Health Book Collective (publisher of *Our Bodies, Ourselves*), and CARASA (Committee for Abortion Rights and Against Sterilization Abuse) need to follow the lead of FINNRET (see page 23) and WRRC and add reproductive engineering to their agendas; nationwide women's organizations need to legitimize and demand women's involvement at every level of the decision-making process on these issues, from hospital ethics committees to insurance review boards.

A women's coalition *may* press to delay or halt research funding for such techniques as artificial wombs or cloning until there has been more public debate about the ethical questions involved; the consequences of rushing are too great. Collecting stories of personal experiences and establishing support groups may well turn out to be a far more appropriate apparatus for making decisions about reproductive issues than the hierarchical procedures that force these issues into the rigid, artificial dialog of traditional politics.

The technologies that encourage the invasion of privacy—two-way cable TV, credit databases, electronic funds transfer permitting real-time surveillance of an individual—demand similar debate about who will control them. In some cases, these implications are dangerously overt: information about liberal and leftist politicians, public figures and reformers was illegally collected for many years by the Los Angeles Police Department Public Disorder Intelligence Division (disbanded as part of a settlement of a suit brought by the American Civil Liberties Union in 1984), under the rubric of preventing terrorist acts; the information was diverted to a computer database owned by Western Goals, a privately supported, extreme right-wing organization connected with the John Birch Society.[2] In other cases, the implications are more subtle: the possibility of correlating purchases made with commercials watched to obtain marketing data, or of searching computerized library circulation records to match up readers with the books they've read. In either case, the implications are troublesome to anyone committed to a free society.

Athough only constant vigilance and legal punishment can prevent abuses like the LAPD case, some of the more subtle abuses can be corrected fairly easily. Just because computers make it easy to collect data, there is no reason it has to be collected: once a book has been returned to the library, the borrower's name can be expunged, leaving only a statistical record showing the number of times a book has been checked out.

Correcting other abuses has a higher price tag attached.

Available encryption (data-scrambling) technologies make it difficult to decode information acquired by tapping a line, but no system provides absolute protection.[3] So far only organizations electronically transmitting large amounts of money, classified data or proprietary material even bother with data security; many more organizations and individuals should be worrying about it. The rash of "hackers" breaking into computer systems shows that almost all unencrypted databases are terribly vulnerable to interception and alteration. A combination of technical research to bring down encryption costs, legislative pressure to provide adequate security for all databases, and public demand to strip identifying name and source information automatically from such data streams as two-way television or videotex access (billing information can be separated from search data) would go far to prevent abuses. As a technology, privacy protection is susceptible to market demand proving that people are willing to pay for it; women should organize a response to that demand.

The domesticated city

It is more than ironic that computer technology, inherently nonlinear, simultaneous and random, ends up reinforcing hierarchical, centralized patterns of work. The infusion of women into the labor force may redirect the use of computers and other technologies to humanize the structure of work itself. Working patterns must be made more responsive to women's needs (and, ultimately, men's) for a more flexible day and a more intermittent employment history. Given the demands of childbearing and childrearing, the increased likelihood of multiple career changes, and the need to replace hazardous and repetitive tasks with creative and challenging ones, new technology could enhance worklife in ways only dreamed of before. But given the existing rationale for implementing technology in the workplace—cutting costs and improving productivity by replacing human workers with machines—women have a rough road ahead.

Decentralized worksites for computer users and electronics assemblers offer an intermediate alternative between telecommuting from the isolation of a home and driving long distances to work. Such worksites could be shared by employees from a number of different firms, could provide day care on site, and would require only facility maintenance. While it would be preferable for women to own and develop such sites, it is more realistic to expect that real estate management firms will develop them in a manner similar to the suite-sharing so popular with lawyers. (A different lawyer or company rents each office and corresponding secretarial desk in a suite, but all the renters share the law library, kitchen, conference room, copying machine and lobby, and pay a portion of the receptionist's and janitor's wages.)

Such sites, scattered throughout many neighborhoods, co-located in large apartment buildings or condominium complexes, or installed in schools or public buildings no longer needed by cities, would reduce commuting times, offer essential social interaction, allocate overhead costs to the company instead of the worker, and be reviewable for environmental compliance. To put this concept into effect, women may need to lobby for changes in zoning and building requirements, arrange financing through lending institutions, devise equitable cost-sharing schemes, and encourage employers to revise their outmoded ways of thinking of the workplace as either a "headquarters" operation or a matter of "putting out" work to individuals. The technology is already available: a terminal and telephone modem is all it takes.

There is no reason, of course, that men couldn't also work at a decentralized station—and handle day care responsibilities as well. These sites would also open up new service jobs, from errand-runners who would serve workers at multiple sites, to combined child and adult day care facilities at an increased number of small, decentralized locations.

Technology promises expanded self-sufficiency for the disabled, allowing the blind to see, the deaf to hear, and the physically challenged to move around. To analyze the ways in which the physical environment creates needless barriers for women, we should pay attention to demands by the handicapped for a barrier-free environment: ramps for wheelchair access permit baby stroller access as well.

Women should also design new technology for the home,

especially technology that makes children, the elderly and men more self-sufficient, thus reducing women's routine caretaking functions. In a song by the "Fathers' Home Defense Hardware Team" on *A Prairie Home Companion* radio broadcast, men sang their praises to household technology by souping up their vacuum cleaners and putting new motors in their Cuisinarts.[4] Home technologies that are too breakable, too dangerous or too difficult for children to operate can be re-invented for simplicity, safety and sturdiness. Certainly, if we can invent child-proof scissors and flameproof pajamas, we can invent a child-proof knife and a stove that can't start a fire or burn someone. (A circuit between a smoke detector and burner knobs on the stove would take care of the former, while a device that shuts off a burner when it no longer senses the weight of a pot or pan might accomplish the latter.)

Multi-purpose home robots, which are technically feasible by the end of the century, need a great deal of research to bring down their projected cost and increase their usefulness before they can be considered more than another expensive toy. Who would pay $8000 for a robotic vacuum cleaner? $3500? $2500?[5] Unless women become involved in robotics design, robots will be useless and silly at best; at worst, they will express the self-indulgent fantasies of their creators in a new form of technological tyranny. Let's hear it for a robot that can pick up and put away clothes and toys (bar-code items with their storage location, perhaps). It's fine if that robot is also able to rake the lawn, mop the floor, make the beds, dust the furniture, and take out the garbage, without being reminded, but let's leave reading bedtime stories to children as something for people to do.

While we may need to wait for GABe's Self-Cleaning House to wash clothes while they're in the closet or dishes while they're in the cupboard, a little thought about what women need and want would infuse household technology with reasonable intention instead of silly gimmicks, such as finding fourteen different ways to say "chop" to justify a 14-speed blender, or painting computers pink to sell them to women.

Large-scale changes in the domesticated city, such as replacing centralized utilities with decentralized sources of energy, from solar water heaters to photovoltaic cells, will require tremendous political pressure on all levels, including pressure for federally or in the UK state-funded research on these topics instead of on nuclear fusion or bringing power down from solar collectors in outer space. (How many people can launch their own rocket?) Again, as an alternative to individually owned or installed units, neighborhood-scale facilities should be researched.

Reach out and touch someone

The potential of telecommunications technology ranges far beyond decentralized computer workstations. *Limited* applications of videotex or teletext shopping services might offer some savings in energy and time: price comparison, reviewing consumers' guides before making a major purchase, handling routine purchases, and making it easier for rural customers to order from laser-disc video catalogs. Sears, Roebuck and Company formed a joint venture called Trintex with IBM and CBS, planning to offer a nationwide videotex service with catalog merchandising, interactive videogames, banking and advertising for a mere $30 (!) per month by 1986. These plans, however, have yet to be achieved—not enough people seem to want the services Trintex will offer.

Common sense indicates that women will not willingly substitute vicarious video shopping for seeing, touching or smelling goods. However, should videotex services become a reasonably priced alternative for the consumer and a boon to the retailer, there is a real danger that many outlets will prefer an all-electronic existence, cutting their overhead costs (storefront rent, labor, etc), by relocating to facilities in less expensive but relatively distant areas, as do mail order firms. As a result, shopping by foot may become an even more time-consuming proposition; videotex services would become a self-fulfilling prophecy.

Alert to the potential of videotex services to repattern social interaction in radical ways, women need to prepare an alternative strategy that emphasizes the physically present technology of transportation, architectural design, and urban planning over the physically absent technology of telecommunications. As long as it is reasonably cheap and reasonably quick to move from place to place, telecommunications loses some of its justification. Mixed-used zoning, alternatives to gasoline-powered automobiles, specially designed housing for single mothers and decentralized services would also enhance interaction on city streets, reduce the need for women to provide chauffeur service, and encourage a sense of community that might eventually minimize the need for anonymous computer "chatting." Alliances with neighborhood organizations can prove exceptionally valuable in generating technological change in these areas.

Do bother your pretty little head

Those who control the implementation of technology have often used it to increase the division of labor between head and hand, between male and female, between skilled and unskilled. While it is nearly impossible to reverse the trend toward office and factory automation, women, working with existing unions or forming new ones, can steer its implementation within the workplace. The most radical change required is not technological, but social: the alliance of women on all job levels within each workplace. This old Congress of Industrial Organizations' strategy of organizing all employees in an organization, regardless of occupation or skill, may be a more effective means of combating new technologies than the American Federation of Labor's and the British trade unions' horizontal approach of organizing by trade across many industries.

Computers and robots imply a total reorganization of workflow within a company; their impact extends far beyond the simple loss of jobs to machines. As work is reorganized, tasks not only flow to the machines but are redistributed both up and down the chain to other workers. For instance, the proliferation of computer terminals has required many more middle managers to type, proof and correct their own reports (secretarial work flowing upward); it has also created pools of task-rationalized, word-processing operators whose work is divided between those entering original text and those correcting it (secretarial work flowing downward). Simultaneously, other secretarial tasks have been de-skilled to justify asking each secretary to handle the work of four times as many "bosses" as before. Office automation thus affects clerical, secretarial and managerial employees, often to the detriment of all of them: workloads increase and become less interesting; remuneration remains the same or is lowered, even when productivity increases; and everyone ends up with greater stress.

CAD/CAM systems (computer-aided design/computer-aided manufacturing) have an equally dramatic impact on the shop floor. The engineer or designer does drafting work directly on the computer (the task flows upward); an employee much less experienced than a skilled machinist is competent to push buttons on a machine tool (task flows downward); and a job that previously demanded a skilled craftsworker is executed by a machine (job is de-skilled).[6] To implement technology so that it liberates human potential instead of imprisons it, women must explicitly connect their fates as executives, middle managers, clerical workers, data entry personnel, engineers or shop floor workers with the fates of all the other women in the facility. On-site childcare centers, gyms or interest groups offer opportunities for women to make connections with each other that supersede the relationships imposed by institutionalized job titles.

If they are able to acknowledge that their survival in the workforce is tied to that of those under them, women find decision-making positions can subtly alter the distribution of tasks and the design of technological systems. For example, word-processing tasks can remain decentralized so that every secretary learns to use the machine (gains a new skill), but is not tied to it. Women in personnel can push for career ladders, rewrite and/or open new job descriptions that reward people for learning new technical skills, and insist that retraining opportunities and "outplacement" assistance be available not just to executives, but to workers at all levels whose jobs are lost or de-skilled because of automation. This sense of female identification is critical if we are to prevent technology from shifting the work done by paid female labor (e.g. billing clerks, bank tellers, receptionists) to unpaid female consumers.

A different future altogether

The new math of plus sum technology

To influence the operations of the global assembly line in
Third World nations, we must extend the principal of
identifying with women across occupational (i.e. class) lines to
identifying with women across racial lines. Women in industrial nations are more than just the consumers of goods
produced by women in developing nations. When we look
critically at our relative status within the labor force of each
nation, rather than comparing it to one another's, it is obvious
that we all share a need to gain greater economic independence and social equality, to fulfill our individual talents, and to
live without fear for ourselves and with hope for our children.
Anthropologist Maria Patricia Fernandez Kelly sees an
opportunity here:[7]

> The internalization of production and the extension of
> complex communications systems are enabling, for the first
> time in history, the creation of a world-wide workforce.
> Women all over the globe share now a common experience,
> the result of their similar position in the world of
> production. And this may yet provide the basis for new
> forms of organization and strengthened solidarity in the
> future.

To realize this possibility, we must learn to exploit satellite
and computer technologies for our own ends, be they new
databases, resource banks or channels for exchanging information about educational opportunities, organizing techniques or
alternative work structures. Women who wish to invest their
capital in politically accountable companies can ask mutual
funds to rate companies on the basis of their treatment of
women in the Third World as well as on the products they
manufacture. Women working in such overwhelmingly female
professions as teaching, nursing and social work can insist that
their pension funds be invested in companies that do not
exploit female laborers on the global assembly line. That
precept applies to portions of the global assembly line
operating within the boundaries of industrialized nations as
well as outside them. Restricting minority women to dead-end,

177

low-paying jobs as electronic assemblers or data entry clerks is unjust no matter where it occurs.

As the post-industrial West converts from steel to silicon, women must push their way into job training programs and occupations unofficially designated "for men only." Only while high-technology industries are fluid and in need of a labor force with new skills will women find it possible to gain a foothold on the future.

Repositioning women on the Great Chain of Being

On the premise that we must stay one step ahead in order not to be left one step behind, we must consider technologies on the cutting edge of change. Research on the following science-fiction technologies is creeping toward application; unlike killer satellites, Star Wars defense systems and neutron bombs, whose purpose is unambiguously military, these technologies, some aspects of which are supported with Defense Department funds, portend dramatic commercial developments as well. Along with previously discussed genetic engineering and cloning experiments, the list includes:

1 the use of living cells to perform processing tasks in computers (biochips);
2 the input of sensory signals directly to the brain, bypassing the sense organs;
3 psychic control of equipment, computers or weapons.

Biochips are promoted as the most realistic way to develop computers that mimic the brain's ability to perform parallel-processing tasks. Human beings can think about several aspects of a problem simultaneously but the existing super-computers used for mammoth number-crunching tasks, and even the forthcoming Japanese-built fifth generation units, solve problems in an essentially sequential manner. For example, a computer programmed to play chess must syste-matically evaluate all possible moves and their consequences through several levels of play before it can select its move. A human chess master, on the other hand, sees patterns and strategies and evaluates them without numerical ordering.

Computer scientists want to speed up the solution of complex problems by creating a computer with the artificial intelligence to break problems into several parts and assign the parts to different portions of its "brain" for simultaneous processing.

Having failed so far to breath "life" into dead elements like silicon, these new alchemists seek to harness the information-processing capability of a living cell to a machine.[8] (Loosely speaking information (organization) and entropy (random-ness) are inversely related; in a theoretical sense, a living cell produces information because its metabolic processes reduce entropy.) A successful biochip computer would generate a traumatic downward shift, equivalent to that caused by Copernicus or Newton, in the philosophical position of man, and therefore woman, on the Great Chain of Being. Apart from its theoretical challenge, a biochip computer offers the possibility of solving astronomical and quantum problems considered essential to understanding the origin of the universe and the nature of matter; it also offers an unprece-dented ability to target thousands of outgoing warheads or track thousands of incoming missiles simultaneously.

Direct sensory input to the brain has enormous potential for the handicapped. Scientists are testing a video camera for the blind that would feed a camera signal directly to the optic nerve to stimulate visual images in the cortex. Similar implants translate sound into an electrical signal that stimulates the auditory nerve, permitting the deaf to hear (assuming in each case that the handicap is caused by a malfunction in the sensory organ itself).[9] This very beneficial technology also opens the door to more questionable electrical implants for externally directed mind control or, conversely, the control of other electrical devices by thought. Imagine "watching" a television show in your brain without having a TV set or using your eyes; imagine directing a car by connecting your brain signal output to the steering wheel; imagine being "taught" programmed information that you cannot see or hear for conscious evaluation. Perhaps everyone walking around with headsets from Sony Walkman cassette players affixed to their ears is preparing for this new day, pre-programming them-selves to receive only the information they get from the machine. . . .

179

These high-technology sensory input and output devices are only a stop along the way to a nontechnological means of exerting control over material objects. The psychic techniques that Sally Gearhart posited as a feminist technology in her science fiction book *The Wanderground*[10] have been documented by Michael Rossman in *New Age Blues* as types of research funded by military and intelligence agencies.[11] After all, if Uri Geller can bend spoons, maybe he can bend a few parts inside a Russian missile. A telepath able to "read" cards inside a black box might be able to "read" secret documents locked in a Moscow safe. The chilling possibility that the CIA or National Security Agency would co-opt people who develop extrasensory skills in telepathy, remote viewing, precognition or psychokinesis emphasizes that the central issue for any technology is who controls it.

New technology, new values

Clearly, then, if we want to create a different world, we have to address the design, production, development, dissemination and control of technology. If we allow technology to remain in the hands of those who have used it to exploit the earth, enslave populations and make war, we are lost. If we try to maintain hard-won social victories without incorporating them into physical reality, we, like Sisyphus, will find ourselves rolling the same rock uphill, over and over again.

But we can master the tools, gain the knowledge and use our imaginations to build artifacts that embody justice, as well as convenience, that revalue the female and honor the human spirit, that ensure survival and move beyond it to celebration.

[14]

Conclusion: the future is now

Before we can expect to be successful in changing the process of technological decision-making, we need to unmask the hidden functions of technology in a stratified society. First and foremost, rather than pointing to the future, technology delineates past power relationships between haves and have-nots, whether the delineation has been based on sex, race, class, information access, degree of privacy or control over birth. When have we ever seen a technology praised for erasing class differences or promoting social equality, instead of maintaining the status quo?

"Keeping things the way they have been" is so obviously a primary motivating force behind technological change that the phrase becomes a contradiction in terms. Technology acts instead as a tool for reacting to any social transformations that threaten the old, familiar world. Instead of supporting on-site childcare for working mothers, for instance, the New Right in the United States attempts to co-opt home computers into a mechanism for strengthening the nuclear family. (The Family Opportunity Act, introduced by conservative representative Newt Gingrich (Republican, Georgia) in 1983, would actually have provided tax credits to families buying home computers for business or educational purposes. Computers would "allow working mothers with pre-school children to earn a living while staying at home," Gingrich explained.[1])

This retrogressive component of technology also partially accounts for the development of planned "communities" that defeat the concept of community in their very construction. Urban sprawl slithers across the landscape, while inadequate

181

Now this is especially designed for the author-housewife. It's a combination food and word processor.

Figure 14.1 The perfect tool for mothers working at home. Recommended by the Family Opportunity Act (Creative Computing, *Wayne Kaneshiro, cartoonist*)

or nonexistent public transit discourages "undesirable" elements from entering wealthy residential and business districts. Zoning ordinances and highway routes conspire to segregate economic classes, often brutally bisecting minority communities to keep them from organizing into a single, politicized neighborhood. Coincidentally, freeways prevent the unpleasant reality of poverty-stricken slums from intruding on the consciousness of the rich; what they don't see does not exist. (What they do see through the windshield of a car often does not exist either: New York City has instituted a program to paste decals of curtains, flower pots and kittycats over the broken windows of uninhabited buildings in the South Bronx, a notoriously bad slum). At the same time, the wealthy lock themselves behind radio-operated security gates, video surveillance cameras and photoelectric burglar alarms. Who is the zookeeper and who is in the zoo?

The mixed blessings of new medical technologies are susceptible to similar analysis. By focusing research dollars (and female caretaking energies) on diagnosing illness or prolonging life through high technology, politicians and professionals deflect attention from prenatal care, nutritional programs, preventive medicine, and regulatory efforts to remove carcinogens and toxic wastes from our water, food, soil, and air. The hidden costs of inadequate motor safety, occupational health hazards, lax food and drug standards and a polluted environment are rarely counted in any official cost/benefit study that weighs the expense of improving those conditions; we ignore the loss of "human capital," of what people would have earned had their health not been impaired or their death not been premature, and bemoan instead the cost of cleaning up the environment and burying the dead.[2]

A matter of class

Technological development is even more insidious when its dissemination is clearly determined by class: "them that has, gets." This principle is clearly demonstrated by the distribution of US government disaster aid funds after Hurricane Camille wreaked havoc in the state of Mississippi in 1969. Funds were disbursed to people in proportion to the amount they had lost, even though it was obviously easier for a wealthy, insured homeowner to replace a home and possessions than it was for an unemployed sharecropper. This distribution method, which simply reinforced the previous class structure, parallels the distribution that occurs with new technology.

For example, 70 percent of US public schools in rich districts have computers; only 40 percent of schools in poor ones do. In spite of laws requiring that school districts spend equal amounts per pupil within a state, parents in different districts have formed organizations to raise money for additional hardware and software. Naturally, parents in rich neighborhoods have more money to contribute; they also can afford to purchase home computers to supplement computer instruction in schools.[3] This skewed distribution of computers, coupled with increased telephone charges and the potential

"Oh the usual. What kind of day did you have?"

Figure 14.2 No matter what her job, the "total woman" makes sure her husband has a home-cooked meal every night. . . .
(*Reprinted by permission from* Science Digest, *copyright* © *1980 The Hearst Corporation; all rights reserved*)

creation of videotex information utilities, threatens to create a new class of information have-nots.

The same principle holds true for the allocation of health care funds. In the United States, with no form of national medical insurance, we are more concerned with advanced reproductive engineering for a relatively few, high-income, non-fertile couples than with distributing prenatal services to two million pregnant, low-income women.[4] (Perhaps this is because the question of paternal identity is so much more appealing to male researchers than the issue of maternal health.) Instead of providing contraceptives to sexually active teenagers, we spend money trying promote adolescent "self-discipline and chastity."[5] And we spent millions of dollars on longevity research and prolongation of life through extraordinary medical means, instead of improving the quality of life, especially for elderly widows, whose old age is spent either in isolation or institutions.[6]

The class-defined availability of expensive heart and liver transplants, very few of which are covered by private or public insurance plans, is like reproductive engineering a class-based phenomenon, thus guaranteeing that only a small fraction of the patients who need such high-technology medical help will get it. In the United States this has been accompanied by the formation of a company planning to *sell* kidneys for transplant, apparently at whatever price set by donors (mostly Third World residents).[7]

If class-defined analysis seems irrelevant to women, consider the ever-increasing feminization of poverty. Statistics from 1982 show that more than two-thirds of all adults living in poverty in the United States are women, and that more than half the households defined as poor are headed by single women. The National Advisory Council on Economic Opportunity had predicted that:[8]

All other things being equal, if the proportion of the poor in female-householder families were to continue to increase at the same rate as it did from 1967 to 1978, the poverty population would be composed solely of women and their children before the year 2000.

Class mobility for women now means downward mobility: after divorce, which ends more than one out of three American marriages, the former wife's standard of living drops, while her ex-husband's rises. Thus, every income-related technology, from computer access to transportation alternatives, has an impact on women out of proportion to their numbers in the population. Expensive new technologies, rather than acting as social equalizers, end up preserving and, sometimes, reinforcing existing patterns of social stratification.

185

Maintaining control

One of the other hidden consequences of technology is the fragmenting of issues into apparently unrelated budget categories, paralleling our general division of knowledge into university departments and subjects. Technology has become so complicated that it can be understood only by dividing it into smaller and smaller parts, or at least so we are told. Thus, we put tobacco subsidies into the budget for the Department of Agriculture and research on lung diseases into the National Heart, Lung and Blood Institute, we enter nuclear energy and nuclear weapons as separate line items, and scrupulously separate contraceptive research and hormones for cattle feed. Because this separation makes it difficult to see the relationships between any two fields, it tends to serve those who have a vested interest in any one of them, rather than those whose interest is best served by looking at the whole picture.

Centralized technologies create new vulnerabilities: power failures immobilize a city, and computer breakdowns cripple airplane reservation systems. Agribusiness investment in a limited number of high-yield "miracle" seeds puts the global food supply at risk. (Concentration on only a few strains of each crop has resulted in a loss of genetic diversity, making it possible for one pest or disease to wipe out a significant proportion of the crop overnight.) The continuing technological search for efficiency, security, convenience and profits has a very high price.

In yet another way, new technology subsidizes the status quo. Because of its factual facade, technology supports the myth of rationality, the concept that the important decisions on this earth must be made by clear, calm *minds*, cautiously weighing the evidence in an effort to reach a fair conclusion. The myth of rationality is quite simply that—a myth. To be sure, there are parameters that can be measured more easily in technical fields than in artistic ones, and we have already seen how comforting measurement can be; if you don't know anything else about something, at least you can pretend to know its size.

What the general public doesn't realize is that those

measurements may be either fallible or irrelevant to the real decision being made. Under the cover of fact (e.g. we have 100 missiles, they have 101), totally irrational choices may be selected (e.g. Mutally Assured Destruction as a means of nuclear deterrence), with the public convinced that "cooler heads have prevailed." "Cooler heads" is, of course, a euphemism for male heads; we wouldn't want any emotional female hysteria clouding our judgment of really important issues that will determine the future of the human race, would we? (Women like Indira Gandhi, Golda Meir and Margaret Thatcher, who have climbed the ladder of power, must prove through their willingness to make war that they aren't hampered by sentimentality and dread emotions.)

The very denial of emotion, and its denigration as a sinister female subtext, serves to drain meaning from language. It accounts for the rapid spread of bureaucratese, educationese, acronyms and Newspeak as mechanisms for lying and obfuscation, mechanisms that simultaneously protect the speaker from revealing his own motives and shield reality from view. Techno-chic language further deflates communication as its terse terms enter daily dialog: firmware, on-line, critical mass, countdown, meltdown.

Technological discourse is thus manipulated to deny and devalue the female content in us all. Subtly, then, and not so subtly, supposedly "neutral" technology is subverted to serve the ends of those in power. It is not the technology that is dangerous, it is the people who control it and the system that sustains it, but those distinctions are rapidly becoming too fine to draw. The danger is perhaps most visible when we acknowledge that technological decisions have a moral component—and that women's moral systems are vastly different from men's.

As a society we have yet to learn how *not* to use a technology, even though it is there. Our cultural acquiescence to new technologies extends even to those that far outrun our abilities to comprehend their consequences, allocate them fairly, or make the ethical and moral choices they demand. These larger themes course like subterranean rivers beneath the obvious features of the technological landscape, unless they happen to bubble to the surface in a news story about robot-run factories, or geyser into attention, the way nuclear weapons and babies born with severe birth defects have done.

Putting aside for the moment the question of why women have kept their fingers off the technological trigger, let us ask instead why men are so fascinated with it. "If a thing can be done, why do it?" asked Gertrude Stein. For years her question seemed to be a challenge to attempt only the impossible, but in this context it takes on a different meaning. If we know that something can be achieved, we are obliged to justify its implementation. Why do something just because it can be done? All those technologies that represent a solution in search of a problem ("we've got it, now we've got to figure out what to do with it") should be subjected to Stein's simple, but most rigorous question.

With an indulgent half-smile playing across their faces, women fondly watch their men, husbands or sons, polish the latest car—whether it's a junkyard special or a new Mercedes Benz. "The bigger the boys, the bigger the toys," they murmur to themselves, discounting the implicit acceptance of technological development that phrase implies. Men live in a world of superlatives, where value is ascertained only by outdoing the next guy. "Biggest." "Best." "Most." "Newest." "Longest." "Longest?" Applying that philosophy of phallic supremacy to technology has given us a nuclear weapons build-up beyond sanity, hills strip-sided of timber or strip-mined of coal, gas-guzzling cars, and satellites that enable us to talk to people around the world before we have learned to talk to those around the block.

Men's preoccupation with conquest needs to be countered by instilling nurturing qualities in male children. Nurturance is not a gender-linked capability; society has assigned it to women. It is one that can, and must, be shared with men, if they are to start learning to accept the consequences of their actions. Without nurturing responsibilities, men are free to concentrate on this month's production, this quarter's profit, this year's purchases, and leave their messes for someone else to clean up.

Technology presents numerous moral issues to a society whose moral values are men's values. Carol Gilligan's brilliant research into the way women's sense of ethics differs from men's, favoring personal relationships over male concepts of abstract justice, calls into question every technology that poses an ethical dilemma.[9] To ignore women's learned concern for a network of relationships and their unwillingness to sacrifice the quality of human life to principles of legality or ownership is to tip the scales of technology away from ever meeting women's priorities and needs.

The arrogance of the "technological fix"

One word of caution. It is tempting to think that if women controlled technology, we could change the physical world until a perfect one exists. The arrogance of the "technological fix" for social and political dilemmas has brought other ships aground on the shoals. In the language of logic, a technological fix is a necessary, but not sufficient, condition for change. Ultimately, we cannot solve social problems that need political solutions with software or solar power. But neither can we maintain social change without embedding it firmly into technology and the built environment.

For example, in 1979 many developing nations sought access at the World Administrative Radio Conference (WARC) to satellite orbits and broadcast frequencies. Since the limited number of geostationary orbits have been assigned on a "first come, first served" basis, industrialized nations with technological capability and funds have quickly been occupying all the available "parking slots" in space. At WARC, the United States and other industrialized nations kept suggesting technological arguments and solutions, rather than addressing the inequity of the "them that has, gets" allocation scheme. No advances in satellite technology could possibly solve the political problems of Third World nations lacking the resources to take advantage of them. Nor, as Third World countries clearly recognized, could developing nations communicate as equals in the modern world without satellite technology.[10]

Or consider what ought to be perfectly gender-free job opportunities in new technologies. Why is it that women are paid less than their male counterparts in the computer industry, a business whose period of phenomenal growth has followed the implementation of laws forbidding job discrimination on the basis of sex? Women's jobs are, quite traditionally, concentrated in the lowest-paying areas of data entry and computer operations, while men's jobs are concentrated in the better-paying categories of systems analysis and data processing machine repair.[11] Once again, new technology has overridden legal progress.

The future in our hands

We exempt technology from rigorous political and economic analysis at our own risk. Although it may, at first glance, seem immune from discriminatory intent or effect, surely we have seen that it is not. Its aura of neutrality derives primarily from the language denuded of values that is used to describe it and from the sterile numerical codes used to assert its importance. The very process of mystification has kept it sacrosanct, a temple for engineering priests who have anointed themselves the oracles of the future. It is time to make a change.

Only the current moment—now—separates our past from our future. While we cannot undo our past (unlike space, time runs in only one direction), we can energize ourselves with the knowledge that dealing with the present moment is more than enough; by changing the present we can change the future. To succeed in creating a different technology we must touch the strength within us. We derive that strength from our mothers, from our grandmothers, from all our foremothers who survived in their time. The actions we take today are not for ourselves; they are taken so our daughters and our daughters' daughters will not have to go through what we have gone through. They will have their own, different battles to fight.

Endurance, flexibility, courage, perseverance—women have learned these traits because we needed them to survive. We need them still; the struggle is not yet met; the barricades are not yet down; the future will be ours only if we create it.

APPENDIX
Resource organizations

Women in science and technology issues

Alliance of Women in Architecture
P.O. Box 5136, FDR Station
New York, NY 10022
USA

American Association for the Advancement of Science
   Women's Caucus
   Handicapped in Science Caucus
   National Network of Minority Women in Science
1776 Massachusetts Avenue, NW
Washington, DC 20036
USA

American Association of University Women
Taking Hold of Technology Topic Committee
2401 Virginia Avenue, NW
Washington, DC 20006

American Medical Women's Association
1740 Broadway
New York, NY 10019
USA

Association for Women in Computing
c/o Katherine Kelley
41 Strawberry Circle
Mill Valley, CA 94941
USA

Association for Women in Mathematics
Center for Research on Women
Wellesley College
828 Washington Street
Wellesley, MA 02181
USA

Association for Women in Psychology
Psychology Department
University of California
Davis, CA 95616
USA

Association for Women in Science
1346 Connecticut Avenue, NW
Suite 1122
Washington, DC 20036
USA

Association of Women Geoscientists
P.O. Box 1005
Menlo Park, CA 94025
USA

Association of Women in Architecture
7440 University Drive
St Louis, MO 63130
USA

ASTMS (Association of Scientific, Technical and Managerial Staffs)
79 Camden Road
London NW1 9ES
UK

Bristol Women and Manual Trades
51 Lower Ashley Road
St Agnes
Bristol 2, UK

British Society for Social Responsibility in Science
9 Poland Street
London W1V 3DG
UK

CARASA: Committee for Abortion Rights and Against Sterilization
  Abuse
386 Park Avenue South
New York, NY 10016
USA

Campaign for Nuclear Disarmament
22–24 Underwood Street
London N1, UK

Center for Science in the Public Interest
Women's Committee
1776 Church Street, NW
Washington, DC 20036
USA

Center for Working Life/Arbetslivcentrum
c/o Ewa Gunnarson
Box 5606
11486 Stockholm
Sweden

City Centre (Information Centre for Women Office Workers)
Sophia House
32–35 Featherstone Street
London EC1, UK

Coalition of Labor Union Women
15 Union Square
New York, NY 10003
USA

Coalition to Defend Medical and Reproductive Rights of Women
4079A 24th Street
San Francisco, CA 94114
USA

Committee on Women in Physics
American Physical Society
Department of Physics
Massachusetts Institute of Technology
Cambridge, MA 02138
USA

COMPOW: Committee on the Position of Women
IEEE
United Engineering Center
345 E. 47th Avenue
New York, NY 10017
USA

ComputerTown USA!
People's Computer Company
263 El Camino Real
Menlo Park, CA 94025
USA

Consumer Action Now
355 Lexington Avenue
New York, NY 10017
USA

CREW (European Database on Women)
Rue de Lanvin
1020 Bruxelles
Belgium

Dutch Project on Women and Technology
c/o Wies Arts
Malakkastraat 8
2585 SN Den Haag
Netherlands

East Leeds Women's Workshop
161 Harehills Lane
Leeds LS8 3GE
UK

Engineering Council,
Canberra House
Strand
London WC2
UK

Equal Opportunities Commission
1 Bedford Street
London WC2
UK

EQUALS in Computer Technology
Lawrence Hall of Science
University of California
Berkeley, CA 94720
USA

Feminist Architects Network
c/o AWP
Hungerford House
Victoria Embankment
London, UK

Feminist Library (database)
Hungerford House
Embankment
London WC2
UK

Feminist Women's Health Center
2930 McClure
Oakland, CA 94609
USA

FINNRAGE (Feminist International Network of Resistance to
Reproductive and Genetic Engineering)
P.O. Box 583
Hampstead
London NW3 1RQ
UK

Forum für Medizin und Gesundheitspolitik
Geneisenouster, 2 (Mehnighof)
100 Berlin 61
West Germany

Foundation for Economic Trends (genetic engineering)
1346 Connecticut Avenue, NW
Washington, DC 20036
USA

Friends of the Earth
377 City Road
London EC1, UK

GAMMA (Girls and Mathematics Association)
c/o Girls & Maths Unit
University of London
Institute of Education
58 Gordon Square
London WC1, UK

Girls and Technology Education (GATE) Project
Centre for Science & Mathematics Education
Chelsea College
University of London
Bridges Place
London SW6 4HK, UK

Girls into Science & Technology (GIST)
Manchester Polytechnic
9 Didsbury Park
Manchester M20 0LH, UK

Haringay Women's Training and Education Centre
Lordship Lane
London N17
UK

IFN: International Feminist Network
c/o ISIS
C.P. 301
1227 Carouge/Geneva
Switzerland

Institut for Industriell Miljoforskning
c/o Merete Lie
N 7034 Trondheim
Norway

Institute for Research on Public Policy
Technology and Society Program
2149 Mackay Street
Montreal, Quebec
Canada H3G 2J2

ISIS: Women's International Information and Communications
  Service
P.O. Box 50 (Cornavin)
1211 Geneva 2
Switzerland

ISIS Italy
Via S. Maria dell'Anima 30
Rome
Italy

Labor Occupational Health Program
2521 Channing Way
Berkeley, CA 94720
USA

Late Start (Black Women's Film, Video and Photography Group)
c/o Outwrite
Oxford House
Derbyshire Street
London E2, UK

Leicester Women and Manual Trades
163 Station Road
Ratby
Leicester LE6 0JR, UK

London New Technology Network:
Women's Project
86–100 St Pancras Way
London NW1 9ES, UK

London Women and Manual Trades
52/54 Featherstone Street
London EC1, UK

Math/Science Network
Math/Science Resource Center
Mills College
Oakland, CA 94613
USA

Microsyster
Wesley House
70 Great Queen Street
Kingsway
London WC2, UK

Matrix Feminist Architecture Group
8 Bradbury Street
London N16 8JN, UK

NARAL: National Abortion Rights Action League
1424 K Street, NW
Washington, DC 20005
USA

National Association of Women in Construction
2800 W. Lancaster
Fort Worth, TX 76107
USA

National Council for Research on Women/Database Project
c/o Barabara Parker, Coordinator
Women's Studies Program
Ketchum 30, Campus Box 325
University of Colorado
Boulder, CO 80309
USA

National Women & Computing Network
c/o Microsyster
Wesley House
70 Great Queen Street
Kingsway
London WC2, UK

National Women's Health Network
1302 18th Street, NW
Washington, DC 20036
USA

NATTA: Network for Alternative Technology and Technology
  Assessment
c/o Alternative Technology Group
Faculty of Technology
Open University
Walton Hall
Milton Keynes, Bucks
UK

9 to 5, National Association of Working Women
1224 Huron Road
Cleveland, OH 44115
USA

Public Resource Center
1747 Connecticut Avenue, NW
Washington, DC 20000
USA

Science for the People
897 Main Street
Cambridge, MA 02139
USA

Self-Cleaning House
c/o Frances GABe
Route 5, Box 695
Newberg, OR 97132
USA

Sigma Delta Epsilon, Graduate Women in Science, Inc.
1346 Connecticut Avenue, NW
Washington, DC 20036
USA

Society for Women in Computing
5320 Sears Tower
233 S. Wacker Drive
Chicago, IL 60606
USA

Society of Women Engineers
United Engineering Center
345 E. 47th Street
New York, NY 10017
USA

Society of Women Geographers
1619 New Hampshire Avenue, NW
Washington, DC 20009
USA

Sociologists for Women in Society
Sociology Department
Kresge College
University of California
Santa Cruz, CA 95064
USA

2-Bit™ Software
Suite 210
10150 Sorrento Valley Rd.
San Diego, CA 92121
USA

South West London Women's Electrics & Electronics Workshops
460 Wandsworth Road
London SW8, UK

SWITCH (Scottish Women into the Computing Habit)
c/o Professor Angela M. Bowey
University of Strathclyde
Livingstone Tower
Room 516
Glasgow G1, UK

Martha Ullerstrom
Karl XI Gatan 11B
222 20 LUND
Sweden

WISE (World Information Service on Energy)
52 Acre Lane
London SW2, UK

WISEST (Pressure Group for Women's Access to Technical
Education and Training)
c/o Sylvia Wasserman
68 Marryat Road
London SW19 5BN, UK

WIST (Women into Science & Technology)
Union Office
Imperial College
Prince Consort Road
London SW7, UK

Women and Health Roundtable
Health Research Group
2000 P Street, NW
Washington, DC 20036
USA

Women and Mathematics Education
Department of Education
George Mason University
4400 University Drive
Fairfax, VA 22030
USA

Women and New Technology Project
c/o Miriam Zukas
Dept. of Adult & Continuing Education
University of Leeds
Leeds LS2 9JT, UK

Women and Technology Group
c/o Science Policy Research Unit, Mantell Building
University of Sussex
Brighton, Sussex BN1 9RF
UK

Women and Technology Network
315 South 4th East
Missoula, MT 59801
USA

Women for Life on Earth
2 Bramhill Gardens
London NW5 1JH, UK

Women and Training Group
c/o Ann Cooke
Dept. of Management Studies
Gloucestershire College of Arts and Technology
Oxstalls Lane
Gloucester GL2 9HW, UK

Women & Work Hazards Group
c/o BSSRS
9 Poland Street
London WC1, UK

Women in Computing Group
c/o Anne Lloyd
76a Mount Ararat Road
Richmond, Surrey TW10 6PN
UK

Women in Construction Advisory Group
Southbank House
Black Prince Road
London SE1 7FJ, UK

Women in Information Technology (WITS)
Leave a message on 01 727 7717

Women in Medicine
c/o Annabel Crowe
34 Hunter House Road
Sheffield 11, UK

Women in Science and Engineering
22 Turning Hill Road
Lexington, MA 02171
USA

Women in Solar and Appropriate Technology
2332 E. Madison
Seattle, WA 98112
USA

Women in Solar Energy
P.O. Box 778
Brattleboro, VT 05301
USA

Women in Sync, Women's Video Resource
Unit 5/6 Wharfedale Project
Wharfdale Road
London N1, UK

Women in Telecom (WIT)
c/o Denise McGuire
Ste Office Room 117
Holborn Centre
120 Holborn
London EC1N 2TE, UK

Women into Science and Engineering
c/o Engineering Council and Equal Opportunities Commission
UK

Women's Bureau
US Department of Labor
200 Constitution Avenue
Washington, DC 20210
USA

Women's Computer Centre
Wesley House
70 Great Queen Street
Kingsway
London WC2, UK

Women's Computer Literacy Project and
    National Women's Mailing List
1195 Valencia St.
San Francisco, CA 94110
USA

Women's Engineering Society
25 Fouberts Place
London W1V 2AL, UK

Women's Equity Action League
733 15th Street, NW
Suite 200
Washington, FC. 20005
USA

Women's Film TV & Video Network
79 Wardour Street
London W1, UK

Women's Health Information Centre
52 Featherstone Street
London EC1, UK

Women's Institute for Freedom of the Press and
   Media Report to Women
3306 Ross Place, NW
Washington, DC 20008
USA

Women's Program Center for Astrophysics
60 Garden Street
Cambridge, MA 02138
USA

A Woman's Place
Hungerford House
Embankment Place
London WC2
UK

Women's Technical Institute
1255 Boylstone Street
Boston, MA 02215
USA

Women's Technology Scheme
c/o MTUCURC
24 Hardman Street
Liverpool L19 AX, UK

Women's Technology Training Workshop
Tritech
Thomas Street
Sheffield, UK

WRRIC (Women's Reproductive Rights Information Centre)
52/54 Featherstone Street
London EC1, UK

Alternative investment funds

Calvert Social Investment Fund
1700 Pennsylvania Avenue, NW
Washington, DC 20006
USA

Dreyfus Third Century Fund
600 Madison Avenue
New York, NY 10022
USA

New Alternatives Fund Inc.
295 Northern Boulevard
Great Neck, NY
USA

Pax World Fund Inc.
224 State Street
Portsmouth, NH 03801
USA

Working Assets Money Fund
230 California Street
San Francisco, CA 94111
USA

Notes and references

PART I   New technology, old values

[1]   Introduction: the future is history

1 Rosaldo, M.Z. and Lamphere, L. (eds), *Woman, Culture and Society*, Palo Alto, Cal., Stanford University Press, 1974. Stanley, A., "Daughters of Isis, daughters of Demeter: when women sowed and reaped," *Women's Studies International Quarterly*, vol. 4, no. 3, 1981, pp. 289-304. Tanner, N. and Zihlmann, A., "Women in evolution, part I: innovation and selection in human origins," *Signs*, vol. 1, no. 3, 1976, pp. 585-608. Zihlmann, A., "Women in evolution, part II: subsistence and social organization among early hominids," *Signs*, vol. 4, no. 1, 1978, pp. 4-20.
2 "Lunch with Nick," calculator advertisement, from Toshiba, America Inc., *TWA Ambassador*, 1980, p. 71.
3 Sullivan, K., "The only way to fly," slide shown at speech by astronaut, University of California, San Diego, 8 May 1980.
4 For a discussion of the contrast between feminist and futurist views of tomorrow, see: Dolkart, J. and Hartsock, N., "Feminist visions of the future," *Quest*, vol. 2, no. 1, 1975, pp. 2-6. For complaints about the sexism in futurology, see "Forum," *Omni*, April 1983, p. 14.
5 Merton, R.K., "Foreword," in J. Ellul, *The Technological Society*, New York, Knopf, 1964, p. vi.
6 Fox, L.H., Brody, L. and Tobin, D. (eds), *Women and the Mathematical Mystique*, Baltimore, Johns Hopkins University Press, 1980. Dembart, "Science: Still few chances for women," LAX, 7 March 1984, pp. I-1, 3, 19. See also Libby Curran, "Science education: did she drop out or was she pushed?", in

Brighton Women and Science Group (ed.), *Alice Through the Microscope: The Power of Science over Women's Lives*, London, Virago, 1980; Kathy Overfield, "Dirty fingers, grime and slag heaps: purity and the scientific ethic", in Dale Spender (ed.), *Men's Studies Modified: The Impact of Feminism on the Academic Disciplines*, Pergamon Press, Oxford, Athene Series, 1981; and Alison Kelly (ed.), *The Missing Half: Girls and Science Education*, Manchester, Manchester University Press, 1981.

7 Rytina, N.F., "Earnings of men and women: a look at specific occupations," *Monthly Labor Review*, April 1982, p. 26. "Women in engineering," *Engineering Manpower Bulletin*, American Association of Engineering Societies, no. 68, September 1983.

8 Ferry, G., "WISE campaign for women engineers," *New Scientist*, vol. 12, January 1984, pp. 10-11.

9 Truxal, C., "The woman engineer," *IEEE Spectrum*, April 1983, pp. 58-62.

10 Woolf, V., *Three Guineas*, New York, Harcourt Brace Jovanovich, 1938, p. 60, Harmondsworth, Penguin, 1977.

11 "Fact sheet on the earnings gap: median earnings by sex 1955-1970," US Department of Labor, Employment Standards Administration, Women's Bureau, Washington, DC, February 1972. "Consumer income report," *Current Population Reports, P-60*, US Department of Commerce, Bureau of the Census, Washington, DC, 1983.

12 Angela Coyle, *Redundant Women*, London, The Women's Press, 1984, p. 139.

[2] Private lives, public choices

1 Holmes, H.B., "Reproductive technologies: the birth of a women-centered analysis," in H.B. Holmes, B.B. Hoskins and M. Gross (eds), *Birth Control and Controlling Birth*, Clifton, New Jersey, Humana Press, 1980, pp. 3-20; see also Rothman, B.K., "The meanings of choice in reproduction technology," in R. Arditti, R. Duelli Klein and S. Minden (eds), *Test Tube Women: what future for motherhood?*, London, Pandora Press, 1984.

2 Roche Laboratories advertisement for Librax, "The Smiling Volunteer," *Journal of the American Medical Association*, vol. 227, no. 7, 1974, pp. 814-15.

3 McCabe, B., "Sex discrimination in courtroom: New Jersey task force takes on judicial gender bias," *Los Angeles Times*, 14 December 1983, p. V-8.

4 Jones, Richard P., "Is rape 'normal reaction'? city to judge," *Los*

Angeles Times 4 September 1977, p. IA-6.

5 Mann, C. "Cystic breasts—a condition, not a disease," *Ms.*, April 1983, p. 86.

6 Gilligan, C., *In a Different Voice: Psychological Theory of Women's Development*, Cambridge, Mass., and London, Harvard University Press, 1982.

7 For a discussion of professionalism, see: Bledstein, B.J., *The Culture of Professionalism: The Middle Class and the Development of Higher Education in America*, New York, Norton, 1976. Haskell, T.L., "Power to the experts," *New York Review of Books*, vol. 24, no. 16, 13 October 1977, pp. 28-33.

8 Rich, A., *Of Woman Born: Motherhood as Experience and Institution*, New York, W.W. Norton, 1976, London, Virago Press, 1977; Arditti, R., Duelli Klein, R. and Minden, S. (eds), op. cit.

9 For artificial insemination, see: Rubin, S., "A spermdonor baby grows up," in J. Zimmerman (ed.), *The Technological Woman: Interfacing with Tomorrow*, New York, Praeger, 1983, pp. 211-15. Winters, B., "Engineered conception: the new parenthood", in Zimmerman (ed.), op. cit., pp. 221-2. For gender selection technique, see Shearer, L., "If a boy is what you want," *Parade Magazine*, 8 January 1984, p. 8.

10 Davidson, K., "Nobel sperm bank founder basks in glow of 1st birth," *Los Angeles Times*, 28 February 1982, p. II-1.

11 Mehren, E., "A controversial sperm bank where the women are in charge," *Los Angeles Times*, 6 February 1983, pp. IV-1,10,11. See also Duelli Klein, R., "Doing it ourselves: self-insemination," in R. Arditti, R. Duelli Klein and S. Minden (eds), op. cit., which describes the experience of a group of lesbian women in London taking control of their own sperm "bank"—a household of gay men.

12 Smith, K. "Surrogate motherhood: an interview," in Zimmerman (ed.), op. cit., pp. 216-20.

13 See "Test tube babies and clinics: where are they?", in R. Arditti, R. Duelli Klein and S. Minden (eds), op cit., pp. 52-4.

14 "Amazing births: babies from 'donor eggs'," *Time*, 23 January 1984, p. 30. Nelson, H., "Woman bears a son by embryo transfer," *Los Angeles Times*, 4 February 1984, p. I-1.

15 Choney, S., "Fertility clinic request withdrawn," *San Diego Union*, 8 January 1981, p. B2.

16 Orwell, G., *1984*, New York, Harcourt Brace, 1949, Harmondsworth, Penguin, 1970.

17 Schwartz, T., "The TV pornography boom," *New York Times Magazine*, 13 September 1981, pp. 121-2, 129. QUBE's inter-

active services have since been curtailed because they were not profitable enough. See "Warner curtails QUBE," *Time*, 30 January 1984, p. 66.

18 Salmans, S. "Scanners monitor buying," *New York Times*, 17 August 1981, p. D8.

19 "TV found to stir fear of violence," *Los Angeles Times* 23 April 1979, p. I-4.

20 Moglino, J., "Prisoner within," *All Things Considered*, Washington, DC, National Public Radio, 31 December 1983.

21 Ibid.

[3] The domesticated city

1 See, for example: Piven, F.F. and Cloward, R.A., *The New Class War*, New York, Pantheon Books, 1982, pp. 13-15, 38-65.

2 Rheinhold, R. "Study says technology could transform society," *New York Times*, 14 June 1982, p. A16.

3 Toffler, A., *The Third Wave*, New York, William Morrow, 1980, p. 215, London, Pan Books, 1981.

4 "Women and the family" and "Women and the economy," *WEAL Washington Report*, vol. 12, no. 3, June/July 1983, pp. 1, 3; and Matrix (ed.), *Making Space: Women and the Man-made Environment*, London, Pluto Press, 1984, p. 5: "About one in nine of all households consist of a man *with* a paid job, a woman *without* one and children under the age of 16." Harris, M., *America Now: The Anthropology of a Changing Culture*, New York, Simon & Schuster, 1981, p. 97.

5 Gutek, B.A., "Women's work in the office of the future," in J. Zimmerman (ed.), *The Technological Woman: Interfacing with Tomorrow*, New York, Praeger, 1983, pp. 159-68.

6 Rytina, N.F., "Earnings of men and women: a look at specific occupations," *Monthly Labor Review*, April 1983, pp. 25-31.

7 For this and the following paragraph, see: Morales, R., "Cold shoulder on a hot stove," in Zimmerman (ed.), pp. 169-80. Mattera, P., "Home computer sweatshop," *The Nation*, 2 April, 1983, pp. 390-2.

8 Morales, op. cit., pp. 173-9. " 'Worksteaders' clean up," *Newsweek*, 9 January 1984, pp. 86-7. Katz, N. "Join the future now: women and work in the electronics industry," San Francisco State University, 1981, photocopy. Ursula Huws discusses union participation in the UK in her book *The New Homeworkers*, London, Low Pay Unit, 1984.

9 Among the many excellent sources for women's work in the home: Bose, C.E. and Bereano, P.L., "Household technologies:

burden or blessing?" in Zimmerman (ed.), op. cit., pp. 83-93, Strasser, S., *Never Done: A History of American Housework*, New York, Pantheon Books, 1982. Oakley, A., *Woman's Work: The Houswife Past and Present*, New York, Vintage Books, 1974. Cowan, R.S., *More Work for Mother: The Ironies of Household Technology from the Open Hearth to the Microwave*, New York, Basic Books, 1983.

10 The most oft-cited study is Vanek, J., "Time spent on housework," *Scientific American*, vol. 231, 1974, pp. 116-20. See also: Berk, S.F., "The household as workplace: wives, husbands and children," in G. Wekerle *et al.* (eds), *New Space for Women*, Boulder, Colorado, Westview Press, 1980, pp. 65-81.

11 Berk, op. cit. Markusen, A.R., "The lonely squandering of urban time," in Zimmerman (ed.), op. cit., p. 95. Brozan, N., "Men and housework: do they or don't they?," *New York Times*, 1 November 1980, p. 52. The figures for the UK for 1975 show women performing 73 percent of domestic labor: see G. Thomas and C. Zmroczek, "Household technology—'liberation' of women from the home?," in P. Close and R. Collins (eds), *Family and Economy in Modern Society*, London, Macmillan, 1985.

12 Markusen, op. cit., p. 97. Hayden, D., *The Grand Domestic Revolution: A History of Feminist Designs for American Homes, Neighborhoods, and Cities*, Cambridge, Mass., MIT Press, 1981. Rock, C., Torre, S. and Wright, G., "The appropriation of the house: changes in house design and concepts of domesticity," in Wekerle *et al.* (eds), op. cit., pp. 83-100.

13 GABe, F., "The GABe self-cleaning house," in Zimmerman (ed.), op. cit., pp. 75-82.

14 "Bonjour," script of radio advertisement for Atari 400 home computer, supplied by Atari Inc., January 1984.

15 Smith, J., *Something Old, Something New, Something Borrowed, Something Due: Women and Appropriate Technology*, Missoula, Montana, Women and Technology Project, 1978. Smith, J., "Women and appropriate technology: a feminist assessment," in Zimmerman (ed.), op. cit., pp. 65-70.

16 Reprinted in Warnock, D., "What growthmania does to women and the environment," in newsletter from Feminist Resources on Energy and Ecology, Syracuse, New York, 1979.

17 McCormack, M., "A feminist perspective," *Social Policy*, December 1977, p. 18.

18 Lloyd, C.B. (ed.), *Sex, Discrimination, and the Division of Labor*, New York, Columbia University Press, 1975, p. 9.

19 Rytina, N.F., "Earnings of men and women: a look at specific occupations," *Monthly Labor Review*, April 1982, pp. 25-31.

20 "Insurance," "Pensions," "Social Security," *WEAL Washington Report*, vol. 12, no. 3, June/July 1983, pp. 3-5.
21 Greene, B., "How much is a housewife worth?," *Los Angeles Times*, 19 September 1980, p. IV-6, 7.

[4] Reach out and touch someone

1 Galbraith, J.K., *Economics and the Public Purpose*, Boston, Houghton Mifflin, 1973, London, André Deutsch, 1974, p. 33.
2 Bartos, R., "What every marketer should know about women," *Harvard Business Review*, vol. 56, no. 3, 1978, p. 74.
3 "Women: what do they want?," *Dealerscope*, January 1984, p. 36.
4 "Stay-at-home British prefer videos to the pubs," *In Touch* (magazine of the British-Dutch Chamber of Commerce), November 1983.
5 Van Gelder, L., "Modems: close encounters of the computer kind," *Ms.*, September 1983, p. 61.
6 Carpenter, T., "Reach out and access someone," *Village Voice*, 6 September 1983, p. 8.
7 Horwitz, J., "A reluctance to leave home," *Womanews*, October 1983, pp. 18-19.
8 Snell, B., *American Ground Transport: A Proposal for Restructuring the Automobile, Truck, Bus, and Rail Industries*, report presented 26 February 1974 to the Subcommittee on Antitrust and Monopoly of the Senate Committee on the Judiciary, 93rd Cong., 2nd/Sess., 1974, committee print, pp. 26-38. Fischler, S.I., *Moving Millions: An Inside Look at Mass Transit*, New York, Harper & Row, pp. 79-101.
9 Goodman, R., *After the Planners*, New York, Simon & Schuster, 1971, pp. 147-57.
10 Giuliano, G., "Getting there: women and transportation," in J. Zimmerman (ed.), *The Technological Woman: Interfacing with Tomorrow*, New York, Praeger, 1983, pp. 102-12.
11 Statistics from 1978 National Transportation Survey, reported by Cambridge Systematics Inc., "Assessment of national use, choice, and future preference toward the automobile and other modes of transportation," 1980.
12 Giuliano, op. cit., p. 111.
13 Naisbitt, J., *Megatrends: Ten New Directions Transforming Our Lives*, New York, Warner Books, 1982.
14 Hacker, S.L., "The culture of engineering: woman, workplace, and machine," *Women's Studies International Quarterly*, vol. 4, no. 3, 1981, p. 350. Mortensen, R.E., "A plea for self-examination by engineering educators," *The California Engineer*,

March 1975, pp. 19-20.

15 "Women in engineering," *Engineering Manpower Bulletin*, no. 68, American Association of Engineering Societies Inc., September 1983.

16 Hacker, op. cit., pp. 341-53.

17 Hutchins, S.E., "Making choices: women in technical policy-making," in J. Zimmerman (ed.), *Conference Proceedings: Future, Technology and Woman*, San Diego, Calif., Women's Studies Department, San Diego State University, 1983, p. 65.

[5] Don't bother your pretty little head

1 "America rushes to high tech for growth," *Business Week*, 28 March 1983, pp 84-87, 90.

2 Rytina, N.F., "Earnings of men and women: a look at specific occupations," *Monthly Labor Review*, April 1982, p. 25-31.

3 Rytina, op. cit., pp. 26-9.

4 "Consumer income report," *Current Population Reports, P-60*, US Department of Commerce, Bureau of the Census, Washington, DC, 1983. *Employment Gazette*, UK, October 1983.

5 "America rushes to high tech jobs for growth," op. cit. Rothschild, E. "Reagan and the real America," *The New York Review*, 15 February 1981, pp. 12-17.

6 Zimmerman, J., "Women in computing: meeting the challenge in an automated industry," *Interface Age*, vol. 8, no. 12, December 1983, pp. 79, 86-8.

7 Kraft, P., *Programmers and Managers*, New York, Springer Verlag, 1977.

8 Schulz, B., "Programmers seen needing fewer skills," *Computerworld*, 28 July 1980, pp. 1, 6. "Funded by National Science Foundation: project opens computer science jobs to women," *Computerworld*, 28 July 1980, p. 17.

9 Smith, J., *Something Old, Something New, Something Borrowed, Something Due: Women and Appropriate Technology*, Missoula, Montana, Women and Technology Project, 1978.

10 US Department of Health and Human Services, "Potential health hazards of video display terminals," DHSS (NIOSH), no. 81-129, Cincinnati, Ohio, 1981.

11 Gregory, J., "The next move: organizing women in the office," in J. Zimmerman (ed.), *The Technological Woman: Interfacing with Tomorrow*, New York, Praeger, 1983, p. 260.

12 Ibid., pp. 260-72.

13 Quoted in Garson, B., "The electronic sweatshop: scanning the office of the future," *Mother Jones*, vol. 6, no. 6, July 1981, p. 41.

14 Mereson, A. "The new fetal protectionism: women workers are sterilized or lose their jobs," *Civil Liberties*, July 1982, pp. 6-7. See aslo: Petchesky, R., "Workers, reproductive hazards, and the politics of protection: an introduction," *Feminist Studies*, vol. 5, no. 2, Summer 1979, pp. 233-45. Chavkin, W., "Occupational hazards to reproduction: a review essay and annotated bibliography, *Feminist Studies*, vol. 5, no. 2, Summer 1979, pp. 311-25.

15 "Genes on the job," *Science for the People*, November/December 1982, pp. 7-8.

16 Cornish, B. "Robots see, hear, feel," *The Futurist*, August 1981, pp. 11-13. Friedrich, O., "The robot revolution," *Time*, 8 December 1980, pp. 72-83. Rytina, op. cit.

17 Otos, S. and Levy, E., "Word processing: this is not a final draft," in Zimmerman (ed.), *The Technological Woman*, op. cit., p. 152.

18 Citibank, New York, telephone conversation with author's research associate to confirm fees, 24 February 1984. "Citibank relents on rule limiting live-teller access," *Los Angles Times*, 31 May 1983, p. IV-2.

19 All statistics from Rytina, op. cit.

20 Pagano, P., "CAB proposes rules for air reservations," *Los Angeles Times*, 10 February 1984, p. IV-1.

21 Timnick, L., "Electronic bullies," *Psychology Today*, vol. 16, no. 2, February 1982, pp. 10-15.

22 Library administrator, San Diego State University, interview with author's research associate, February 1984.

23 Parker, B., "Summary, October 18, 1982, meeting, National Council Data Base Project," Women's Studies Program, University of Colorado, Boulder, photocopy.

[6]   The bad math of zero sum technology

1 Dublin, T., *Women at Work*, New York, Columbia University Press, 1979, pp. 5, 14-16. Baxautall, R. *et al.* (eds), *America's Working Women*, New York, Random House, 1976, pp. 13-15, 20-21. Oakley, A., *Woman's Work: The Houswife Past and Present*, New York, Vintage Books, 1976, pp. 32-6.

2 Ibid., pp. 35-6.

3 Pinchbeck, J., *Women Workers and the Industrial Revolution*, New York, August M. Kelley, reprinted 1969, p. 4, London, Virago, 1981.

4 Dublin, op. cit., p. 109. Abbott, E., *Women in Industry: A Study in American Economic History*, New York, Arno Press, reprinted 1969, p. 269.

5 Ibid., 279. Dublin, op. cit., p. 66. See also Clark, A., *The*

Working Life of Women in the Seventeenth Century, London, Routledge & Kegan Paul, 1982 (first published 1919).

6 Dublin, op. cit., p. 18.

7 According to Dublin, op. cit., p. 137, "Output per worker averaged across these firms rose by almost 49% from 1836 to 1850, while daily wages increased only 4%."

8 "The instant offshore office," *Business Week*, 15 March 1982, p. 136E.

9 Fernandez-Kelly, M.P., "Gender and industry on Mexico's new frontier," in J. Zimmerman (ed.), *The Technological Woman: Interfacing with Tomorrow*, New York, Praeger, 1983, pp. 18-29.

10 Hourly wages from *Semiconductor International*, February 1982, chart shown in: Fuentes, A. and Ehrenreich, B., *Women in the Global Factory*, INC pamphlet no. 2, Institute for New Communications, New York, South End Press, 1983, p. 9.

11 Morales, R., "Cold solder on a hot stove," in Zimmerman (ed.), op. cit., pp. 169-80.

12 Anderson, Marion, *Neither Jobs Nor Security: Women's Unemployment and the Pentagon Budget*, Lansing, Michigan, Employment Research Associates, 1982.

13 Ibid., p. 1.

14 Erie, S.P., Rein, M. and Wiget, B., "Women and the Reagan revolution: Thermidor for the social welfare economy," paper presented at the annual meeting of the Western Political Science Association, San Diego, Calif., March 1982.

15 Ibid., p. 37. Barnes, M.B., "Government layoffs undermine past affirmative action gains," *Women's Political Times*, April 1982, p. 4.

16 Bumstead, R., "Opening up high technology careers for women," *American Education*, vol. 16, no. 3, April 1980, pp. 25-31.

17 Hacker, S.L., "Sex stratification, technology and organizational change: a longitudinal case study of AT & T," *Social Problems*, vol. 26, no. 5, June 1979, pp. 539-57.

18 Walshok, M., *Blue Collar Women: Pioneers on the Male Frontier*, Garden City, New York, Anchor Books, 1981, pp. 44-5, 206-7.

[7] Machines 3; Angels 0

1 Stanley, A., "Daughters of Isis, daughters of Demeter: when women sowed and reaped," *Women's Studies International Quarterly*, vol. 4, no. 3, 1981, pp. 289-304.

2 Sayre, A., *Rosalind Franklin and DNA*, New York, W.W. Norton, 1975.

3 Lovejoy, A.O., *Great Chain of Being: A Study of the History of*

an Idea, Cambridge, Mass., Harvard University Press, 1936, pp. 59-80.

4 Pope, A., *Essays on Man*, quoted in Lovejoy, op. cit., p. 60.

5 Lovejoy, op. cit., pp. 99-143.

6 Descartes, R., *Principia* III, p. 3.

7 Alic, M., "Women and technology in ancient Alexandria," *Women's Studies International Quarterly*, vol. 4, no. 3, 1981, p. 311.

8 Jenyns, S., "Disquisitions on several subjects, I: 'on the chain of universal being'," in *Works*, 1790 edition, pp. 179-85.

9 Lovejoy, op. cit., pp. 204-7.

10 Pope, A., *Essays on Man, Epistle IV*, 11

11 Lowe, M., "Sex differences, science, and society," in J. Zimmerman (ed.), *The Technological Woman: Interfacing with Tomorrow*, New York, Praeger, 1983, p. 10.

12 "Time's Man of the Year for 1982," *Time*, 3 January 1983, p. 3.

13 "Computer 'snitched' on absent youths, they shoot it 48 times," *Los Angeles Times*, 18 December 1983, p. I-27.

14 Quoted in Davidson, K., "San Diego's in the running for joint computer research center," *Los Angeles Times*, 13 May 1983, p. II-9.

15 Boulding, K., *The Image*, Ann Arbor, University of Michigan Press, 1956.

16 ELIZA, a program invented by Joseph Weizenbaum at the Massachusetts Institute of Technology acted as a computer therapist by matching a statement entered at the keyboard, such as "I'm worried about my dog," with a screen question, such as "Tell me more about your dog." The program was enormously popular.

17 Dreyfus, H.L., "Computer technology—its limitations and dangers," a speech given at Logon '83: Technology, Mythology, and Literacy in the New Age, Montana State University, Bozeman, August 1983. For more information, see Dreyfus, H.L., *What Computers Can't Do: A Critique of Artificial Reason*, New York, Harper & Row, 1972.

18 Wilbur, E., of Arthur D. Little Inc., quoted in Wolkomir, R., "Robots at home," *OMNI*, April 1983, p. 75.

19 Chamberlin, L.J. "Facing up to robotation," *USA Today*, November 1982, p. 32.

20 Wolkomir, op. cit., p. 75.

21 Bushnell, N., of Androbot Inc., quoted in Wolkomir, op. cit., p. 76.

22 "It's a geep," *Time*, 27 January 1984, p. 71.

23 Diamond vs. Chakrabarty, 1980. See O'Rourke, C.L., "Science

policy: the Chakrabarty decision," *Environment*, vol. 22, no. 6, 1980, pp. 4-5, 42.

24 May, L., "Battle over plant gene splicing heats up," *Los Angeles Times*, 3 November 1983, p. IB-1, 3.

25 For more information, see Rifkin, J., *Algeny*, New York, Viking Press, 1983.

26 Smythe, D.W., "Communications: the blind spot of Western Marxism," Communications Department, Simon Fraser University, Burnaby, British Columbia, 1976, photocopy.

27 Goodman, Ellen, "Cabbage Patch dolls," *Nightline*, ABC News, 1 December 1983.

28 Mason, R., with Jennings, L. and Evans, R., *Xanadu: The Computerized Home of Tomorrow and How It Can Be Yours TODAY!*, Washington, DC, Acropolis Books, 1983.

29 Forino, M., quoted in Chin, K., "Hubotics unwraps robot designed for the home," *Infoworld*, 13 February 1984, p. 67.

30 Mason, op. cit., p. 15.

31 *Williamsburg: Visit Virginia's Historic Triangle*, brochure published by Williamsburg Area Chamber of Commerce, Williamsburg, Virginia, acquired 1983.

PART II The invisible tyranny of things

[8] Progress as product

1 Voltaire, *Candide*, trans. L. Bair, New York, Bantam Books, 1959, p. 117, Harmondsworth, Penguin, 1970. Voltaire used the character of Dr Pangloss to mock Leibniz's philosophical optimism that "everything is for the best in this best of all possible worlds."

2 Dickson, P., *Think Tanks*, New York, Atheneum, 1971, pp. 310-47.

3 Ibid., p. 311.

4 Huckle, P., "Feminism: a catalyst for the future," in J. Zimmerman (ed.), *The Technological Woman: Interfacing with Tomorrow*, New York, Praeger, 1983, pp. 283-4.

5 Dickson, op. cit., pp. 345-47.

6 Dickson, op. cit., pp. 312-18.

7 Okin, S.M., *Women in Western Political Thought*, Princeton, New Jersey, Princeton University Press, 1979, pp. 234-5, London, Virago, 1980.

8 King, Y., "Feminism and ecology: a course description," in brochure, *Goddard College Social Ecology Summer Program*,

Plainfield, Vermont, 1 June-21 August, 1981.

9 Watts, A., *Nature, Man, and Woman*, New York, Pantheon Books, 1958, p. 55.
10 See for example Parker, R., *The Subversive Stitch Embroidery and the Making of the Feminine*, London, The Women's Press, 1984.
11 Martin, D., "One hundred years hence . . . ho-hum, yet another day," *Los Angeles Times Home Magazine*, 31 August 1980, p. 24.
12 Lowe, M., "Sex differences, science and society," in Zimmerman (ed.), op. cit., pp. 15-16.
13 Wilson, E.O., *Sociobiology: The New Synthesis*, Cambridge, Mass., Belknap Press of Harvard University Press, 1975.
14 Barash, D.P., *Sociobiology and Behavior*, New York, Elsevier North-Holland, 1977, p. 283, London, Hodder & Stoughton, 1982.
15 Spring, S.P. and Deutsch, G., *Left Brain, Right Brain*, San Francisco, W.H. Freeman, 1981, pp. 43-6, 121-30.
16 Benbow, C. and Stanley, J.C., "Sex differences in mathematical ability: fact or artifact?," *Science*, vol. 210, no. 12, 1980, pp. 1262-4.
17 Beckwith, J. and Durkin, J., "Science and the attack on women: girls, boys, and math," *Science for the People*, vol. 13, no. 5, 1981, pp. 6-9, 32-5.
18 Lowe, op. cit., p. 16.
19 Ibid.
20 Jurney, D., "Update report," *Media Report to Women*, vol. 12, no. 1, January/February 1984, p. 5.

[9]   What are rights without means?

1 Davis, R.H., *Life in the Iron Mills, or the Korl Woman*, 1st edn, 4th printing, New York, The Feminist Press, 1972, first published in the *Atlantic Monthly*, April 1861.
2 This discussion applies only to monuments. For some of the many excellent homes, offices and public buildings women have designed, see: Torre, S., (ed.), *Women in American Architecture: A Historic and Contemporary Perspective*, New York, Whitney Library of Design, 1977. Cole, D., *From Tipi to Skyscraper: A History of Women in Architecture*, Boston, MIT Press, 1973.
3 Torre, op. cit., p. 11. Cole, op. cit., pp. 8-9. Stanley, A., "From Africa to America: Black women inventors," in Zimmerman (ed.), *The Technological Woman: Interfacing with Tomorrow*, New York, Praeger, 1983, p. 57. Archambault, J., "Women: inventing the wheel," *Conference Proceedings: Future, Technology, and Woman*, San Diego, Women's Studies Depart-

ment, San Diego State University, 1981, pp. 39-40.

4 Rytina, N.F., "Earnings of men and women: a look at specific occupations," *Monthly Labor Review*, April 1982, pp. 25–31. Matrix, *Making Space*, London, Pluto Press, 1984, p. 2.

5 Irvin, H.D., "The machine in utopia: Shaker women and technology," *Women's Studies International Quarterly*, vol. 4, no. 3, 1981, p. 315. Hayden, D., "Redesigning the domestic workplace," in G. Wekerle *et al.* (eds), *New Space for Women*, Boulder, Colorado, Westview Press, 1980, p. 115.

6 Stanley, op. cit., pp. 61-2.

7 Leff, N., "Historic chart relating architectural projects to general and women's history in the United States," in Torre (ed.), op. cit., p. 205.

8 Irvin, op. cit., pp. 314-15.

9 Weiser, M.P.L. and Arbeiter, J.S., *Womanlist*, New York, Atheneum, 1981, p. 106.

10 Stanley, op. cit., p. 60.

11 Slocum, S., "Woman the gatherer: male bias in anthropology," in R.R. Reiter (ed.), *Toward an Anthropology of Women*, New York, Monthly Review Press, 1975. Tanner, N. and Zihlmann, A., "Women in evolution part I: innovation and selection in human origins," *Signs*, vol. 1, pp. 585-608. Bleier, R., "The universal and eternal subordinance of women? The arts and sciences of theory making their feminist deconstructions," paper presented at Women's Studies: Its Impact on Society, Technology and the Arts, Milwaukee, Wisconsin, October 1981.

12 Stanley, A., "Daughters of Isis, daughters of Demeter: when women sowed and reaped," *Women's Studies International Quarterly*, vol. 4, no. 3, 1981, pp. 289-304.

13 Alic, M., "Women and technology in ancient Alexandria: Maria and Hypatia," *Women's Studies International Quarterly*, vol. 4, no. 3, 1981, pp. 307, 309-10.

14 Weiser and Arbeiter, op. cit., pp. 105-6.

15 Rytina, op. cit.

16 "Video: Donkey Kong goes to Harvard," *Time*, 6 June 1983, p. 77.

17 "Audio comes to video games," *Changing Times*, August 1983, p. 9.

18 Hutchins, S.E., conversation with author, 1982.

19 Margulies, L., " 'Custer's Revenge' is discontinued," *Los Angeles Times*, 12 January 1983, p. VI-7.

20 Sindermann, C.J., *Winning the Games Scientists Play*, New York, Plenum Press, 1982, pp. 204, 206-7.

21 Emerson, S., "Bambi meets Godzilla: life in the corporate

jungle," in Zimmerman (ed.), op. cit., pp. 201-6.

22 Lakoff, R., "Doubletalk: sexism in tech talk," in Zimmerman (ed.), op. cit., pp. 38-43.

23 Ibid., p. 41.

24 Griffin, S., *Woman and Nature: The Roaring Inside Her*, New York, Harper & Row, 1978, p. 226.

[10] The politics of technology

1 For the menstruation comment, see Malebranche, quoted in O'Faolain, J. and Martines, L., *Not in God's Image*, New York, Harper & Row, 1973, p. 246, London, Virago, 1979. For the comment about the intelligence of Blacks, see the entry for Nobel Laureate William Shockley in Wallechinsky, D. and Irving W., *The People's Almanac*, Garden City, New York, Doubleday, 1975, p. 1108.

2 Griffin, S., *Woman and Nature: The Roaring Inside Her*, New York, Harper & Row, 1978, pp. 125-6.

3 Rogers, M., "Selling psych-out software," *Newsweek*, 16 January 1984, p. 52.

4 Kevles, B., "Botanist honored for genetic discovery," *Los Angeles Times*, 2 November 1983, p. V-2.

5 GABe, F., "The GABe self-cleaning house," in J. Zimmerman (ed.), *The Technological Woman: Interfacing with Tomorrow*, New York, Praeger, 1983, pp. 75-82.

6 Hacker, S.L., "The culture of engineering: woman, workplace and machine," *Women's Studies International Quarterly*, vol. 4, no. 3, 1981, pp. 341-53.

7 Mortensen, R.E., "A plea for self-examination by engineering educators," *The California Engineer*, March 1975, pp. 19-20.

8 Kuhn, T., *The Structure of Scientific Revolutions*, 2nd edn, Chicago, University of Chicago Press, 1970, pp. 1-9.

9 Zimmerman, B. *et al.*, "People's science," in R. Arditti *et al.* (eds), *Science and Liberation*, Boston, South End Press, 1980, pp. 302-5. Schwartz, C., "Scholars for dollars," in ibid., pp. 171-85.

10 Kiefer, I., *Global Jigsaw Puzzle: The Story of Continental Drift*, New York, Atheneum, 1978, p. 4-5, 9, 14-19.

11 Kanter, R.M., *Men and Women of the Corporation*, New York, Basic Books, 1977, p. 47.

12 Zimmerman, B. *et al.*, op. cit. Yaes, R., "The scientific establishment," in Arditti *et al.* (eds), op. cit., pp. 271-18, 232-6.

13 Shapley, D., "Obstacles to women in science," *Impact of Science on Society*, vol. 25, no. 2, April/June 1975, pp. 120-2.

14 "More than $5 million awarded to woman in GM X-car lawsuit," *Los Angeles Times*, 10 December 1983, p. I-20.

15 "Jury in GM case awards $5,250,000 to injured woman," *Wall Street Journal*, 12 December 1983, p. 5.

16 Mills, C.W., *The Power Elite*, New York and Oxford, Oxford University Press, 1956, pp. 212-19.

17 Tobias, S., Goudinoff, P., Leader, S. and Leader, S., *What Kind of Guns Are they Buying With Your Butter?*, New York, William Morrow, 1982, pp. 249-60. Leader, S. *et al.*, "An intelligent woman's guide to defense," *Ms.*, March 1983, p. 60.

18 Flanigan, J., "Our defense industry needs strong dose of capitalism," *Los Angeles Times*, 15 January 1984, p. VI-1.

19 Melman, S., *The Permanent War Economy: American Capitalism in Decline*, New York, Simon & Schuster, 1974, pp. 241-2.

20 "Federal budget outlays: defense," *Los Angeles Times*, 2 February 1984, p. I-13. Wilson, J.O., "New budget reaffirms the shift in government priorities under Reagan," *Los Angeles Times*, 12 February 1984, p. V-3. Scheirer, B., Small Business Administration, US Department of Commerce, Washington, DC, telephone conversation with author's research associate, 23 February 1984.

21 For UK figures on defense spending, see *Statement on the Defense Estimates* (2), London, HMSO, 1984, p. 9.

22 Arditti *et al.* (eds), op. cit., pp. 2-3.

23 Sivard, R.L., *World Military and Social Expenditures 1981*, Leesburg, Virginia, World Priorities, 1981, p. 18.

24 Figures derived from Anderson, Marion, *Neither Jobs nor Security: Women's Unemployment and the Pentagon Budget*, Lansing, Michigan, Employment Research Associates, 1982.

25 Sivard, op. cit., p. 20.

26 Arditti, *et al.* (eds), op. cit., p. 3.

27 "A *Newsweek* poll on the gender gap: sharp differences," *Newsweek*, 19 September 1983, p. 40.

28 Murphy, B., *The World Wired Up: Unscrambling the New Communications Puzzle*, London, Comedia Publishing, 1983, pp. 30-4, 44. Smith, R.L., *The Wired Nation*, New York, Harper & Row, 1972, pp. 1-9.

29 Crook, D., "Channels merge for cable arts," *Los Angeles Times*, 31 January 1984, p. VI-1,8. "Warner curtails QUBE," *Time*, 30 January 1984, p. 66.

30 Murphy, op. cit., pp. 33, 44.

31 Koughan, M., "The state of the revolution 1982," *Channels*, December/January 1981, p. 24.

32 For a discussion of the economic points raised in this chapter, see

Harris, M., *America Now: The Anthropology of a Changing Culture*, New York, Simon & Schuster, 1981.

[11] Qui bono?

1 "Recipe Chef," promotional letter sent to 2-Bit Software, 1 February 1984.
2 Dechard, B.S., *The Women's Movement: Political, Socioeconomic, and Psychological Issues*, 3rd edn, New York, Harper & Row, 1983, p. 377.
3 Ehrenreich, B. and Stallard, K., "The nouveau poor," *Ms.*, August 1982, p. 217.
4 Moss, A., "Social security: pension plans shortchange women," *Women's Political Times*, vol. 8, no. 2, 1983 p. 2.
5 "Consumer income report," *Current Population Reports, P-60*, US Department of Commerce, Bureau of the Census, Washington, DC, 1983.
6 Lewin, L.C., *Report from Iron Mountain on the Possibility and Desirability of Peace*, New York, Dial Press, 1967, pp. 57-64.
7 Richte, P. "Software publishers brace for a shakeout," *Los Angeles Times*, 27 February 1984, p. IV-1, 4, 7, 8.

PART III Tomorrow is a woman's issue

[12] Taking charge of tomorrow

1 Ciotti, P., "Revenge of the nerds," *California Magazine*, vol. 7, no. 7, July 1982, pp. 73-7, 127-34.
2 Charlotte Whitton, mayor of Ottawa, Ontario, June 1963, quoted in Carle, L.W., "Women talking about themselves," *New York Times*, 26 November, 1977.
3 Griffin, S., *Woman and Nature: The Roaring Inside Her*, New York, Harper & Row, 1978, p. 119.
4 Kelly, A. and Weinreich-Haste, H., "Science is for girls?," *Women's Studies International Quarterly*, vol. 2, no. 3, 1979, pp. 286-93.
5 Kreinberg, N. and Stage, E., "EQUALS in computer technology," in J. Zimmerman (ed.), *The Technological Woman: Interfacing with Tomorrow*, New York, Praeger, 1983, pp. 251-9. Ferry, G., "WISE campaign for women engineers," *New Scientist*, vol. 12, January 1984, pp. 10-11.
6 "Briefing," *New York Times*, 16 September 1982, p. A10.
7 Frances GABe, Self-Cleaning House, Route 5, Box 695,

Newberg, OR 97132.
8 "Episode #61," *Wall Street Journal Report*, New York, Independent Network News, 25-27 November, 1983.
9 Miller, J.B., *Toward a New Psychology of Women*, Boston, Beacon Press, 1976, Harmondsworth, Penguin, 1978.

[13] A different future altogether

1 Nelson, H., "Blue Shield may cover Stanford heart surgery," *Los Angeles Times*, 2 February 1984, p. I-1, 22.
2 Sappell, J., "Detective in spying case linked to Birch leader," *Los Angeles Times*, 24 May 1983, p. I-1, 3, 14.
3 Bernhard, R., "Breaking system security," *IEEE SPectrum*, June 1982, p. 24-31.
4 "The father's Home Defense Hardware team," radio sketch, *A Prairie Home Companion*, National Public Radio, 20 August 1983.
5 "Home robots are coming," *Business Week*, 13 December 1982, pp. 62-3.
6 Shaiken, H., "Numerical control of work: workers and automation in the computer age," paper presented at the Conference on Technological Change, Wayne State University, Detroit, October/November 1979.
7 Fernandez-Kelly, M.P., "Gender and industry on Mexico's new frontier," in J. Zimmerman (ed.), *The Technological Woman: Interfacing with Tomorrow*, New York, Praeger, 1983, p. 28.
8 Dembart, L. "Molecular computer: science or fiction?," *Los Angeles Times*, 30 October 1983, p. I-3, 12, 13.
9 Brody, R., "Breakthroughs help deaf-blind person to see and to hear" *Science Digest*, vol. 88, October 1980, p. 51. "Artificial ear," CBS-TV, San Diego, 27 February 1984.
10 Gearhart, S., *The Wanderground: Stories of the Hill Women*, Watertown, Mass., Persephone Press, 1979.
11 Rossman, M., *New Age Blues: On the Politics of Consciousness*, New York, E.P. Dutton, 1979, pp. 213-24. See also: "An E.S.P. gap: exploring psychic weapons," *Time*, 23 January 1984, p. 17. "Mind wars," *Nightline*, ABC News, 15 February 1984.

[14] Conclusion: the future is now

1 Representative Newt Gingrich (Republican, Georgia) quoted in Mattera, Philip, "Home computer sweatshops," *The Nation*, 2 Februarty 1983, p. 392.
2 Harris, M., *America .Now: The Anthropology of a Changing Culture*, New York, Simon & Schuster, 1981, p. 67.

3 Markoff, J., "Who's in front?," *Infoworld*, vol. 5, no. 44, 31 October 1983, pp. 32-3. Wierzbicki, B., "Micro haves and have-nots," *Infoworld*, vol. 5, no. 44, 31 October 1983, pp. 36-8.

4 Parker, A., "Juggling healthcare technology and women's needs," in J. Zimmerman (ed.), *The Technological Woman: Interfacing with Tomorrow*, New York, Praeger, 1983, pp. 242-3.

5 Bros, C. and Marks, P., "Reagan budget singles out women, despite rhetoric," *Women's Political Times*, vol. 7, no. 2, 1982, p. 17.

6 Krier, B.A., "Gray Panthers enraged, attack Reagan policies at convention," *Los Angeles Times*, 31 March 1983, p. V-2.

7 Kaplan, A., " 'Cash market' is no place for trade in vital organs," *Los Angeles Times*, 21 September, p. II-7.

8 Quote and statistics from: "Ehrenreich, B. and Stallard, K., "The nouveau poor," *Ms.*, August 1982, p. 217.

9 Gilligan, C., *In a Different Voice: Psychological Theory of Women's Development*, Cambridge, Mass. and London, Harvard University Press, 1982.

10 Rutkowski, A.M., "Six ad-hoc two: the third world speaks its mind," *Satellite Communications*, March 1980, pp. 22-7.

11 Zimmerman, J., "Women in computing: meeting the challenges in an automated industry," *Interface Age*, December 1983, pp. 79, 86-8.

Index

Index

Gandhi, Indira, 187
Garson, Barbara, 57
Gearhart, Sally, 105, 180
gender determination, 19
gene splicing, 55
General Electric, 97
General Motors, 49, 50, 97, 132
genetic: determinism, 59, 106-7, 124; engineering, 19, 78, 84-5; screening, 16, 59, 86
Gerbner, George, 25
Gilbreth, Lillian, 33
Gilligan, Carol, 17, 188-9
Gingrich, Newt, 181
Giuliano, Genevieve, 51
global assembly line, 177-8
Goodman, Ellen, 87
Graham, Robert, 20
grants, 127, 129-33, 186
Great Chain of Being, 76-7, 79-82, 88
Greene, Catherine Littlefield, 75
Greenham Common, 117
Griffin, Susan, 122, 125, 157
Guthrie, Janet, 104

Hacker, Sally L., 72, 127
hackers, 171
Haringey Women's Training and Education Centre, 72
Harp, Lore, 14
Hayden, Sophia, 110
health care, funding, 184
Hearst, William Randolph, 110
high technology: commercialization of, 97; dangers of, 96; as religion, 100; sexism in, 118; social impacts of, 139-41
high-tech, high-touch, 51
Hitler, Adolf, 86
home control units, 88, 91
Hopi Indians, 54
Hopper, Capt. Grace, USNR, 56
Horwitz, Jamie, 64
Hottentot, 79
household labor, 46; collective, 31-2; content change, 33-6; privatization of, 33-40; worth of unpaid, 40, 61

household technology, 32-3, 39, 88, 172-3; effect on women, 33, 44-6
Hubot, 84, 85, 88
Hudson Institute, 102
Hutchins, Dr. Sandra E., 119
Hypatia, 114

in vitro fertilization (IVF), 19, 21-4, 168
independent contractor, 69
Industrial Age, 73
Industrial Revolution, 66
industry, cottage, 66-8
Information Age, 60-1, 76
information society, access to, 46
Institute for the Future, 30, 101
intuition, 126-7
inventors, women, 3-4, 75, 112-14, 131
investment, 181; socially responsible funds, 164, 177
ISIS, 14
ITT Corp., 97, 119

jargon, 120; in daily life, 186
job: discrimination, 11; rationalization, 57; segregation, 31

Kahn, Herman, 102
Kanter, Rosabeth Moss, 130
Kay, Alan, 117
Kelly, Maria Patricia Fernandez, 177
Kelly, Petra, 143
Kenner, Beatrice, 112
keyword comprehension, 63; *see also* databases
Kistiakowsky, Vera, 14
Kono Tribe, 112
Kuhn, Thomas, 128
Kumeyaay Indian, 112

Lakoff, Robin, 120
Lamaze, 17
language, sexism in, 8, 117, 118-22
law, sexism in, 36
LeGuin, Ursula, 105
leisure time, 36, 46
lesbians, 19

227

Index

Index

PANDORA PRESS

Pandora Press is a feminist press, an imprint of Routledge & Kegan Paul. Our list is varied — we publish new fiction, reprint fiction, history, biography, autobiography, social issues, humour — written by women and celebrating the lives and achievements of women the world over. For further information about Pandora Press books, please write to the Mailing List Dept. at Pandora Press, 11 New Fetter Lane, London EC4P 4EE or in the USA at 29 West 35th Street, New York, NY 10001.

Some Pandora titles you will enjoy:

CHANGES OF HEART
Reflections on the Theme of Women's Independence

Liz Heron

Using an original format of combining beautiful and incisive prose, interviews with women, and personal pieces about the author's own life, *Changes of Heart* is an unusual, uplifting and thought-provoking foray into the lives of women today.

With strong contextual pieces on the politics and culture which surround and form our consciousnesses, Liz Heron explores how women's lives have been altered by the social changes of the last two decades, and how women's relationships with men and with women have been touched or altered by these changes.
0 86358 028 9p   224pp
General/Social Questions

A WEALTH OF EXPERIENCE
The Lives of Older Women

Edited by Susan Hemmings

It is often hard for people to think of growing older in a positive way, but this book shows the strength and dignity of eighteen women who are now aged between 40 and 65.

These women talk openly about their lives, about the political changes and growth in women's consciousness that they have witnessed and experienced through the twentieth century. *A Wealth of Experience* is a celebration of the achievements of older women, of their ability to survive hardships which are familiar to all women. This book is a patchwork of personal histories and political ideas that reflect some of the best characteristics of oral history such as the release of knowledge and experience of people normally silenced. But it is also an invaluable guide for all women; for older women to identify some common roots and shared causes and for younger women who will one day join their number.
0 86358 031 9p   192pp
General/Social Questions

THE PATIENT PATIENTS
Women and Their Doctors

Helen Roberts

What do doctors think about their patients? And what do women think of their doctors? Helen Roberts investigates the relationship between women and their doctors and sets out to answer such questions as the reasons for women's ill health and the support, or lack of it, they get from their families.

She suggests changes that will benefit both patients and doctors and provides a sensitive portrayal of women, 'The Patient Patients'.

'Nearly every woman will see in these pages a reflection of herself in her relationship with doctors.'

Sheila Kitzinger

0 86358 019 Xp   130pp
Health/Social Questions

BIRTH AND OUR BODIES
Exercises and Meditations for the Childbearing Years and Preparation for Active Birth

Paddy O'Brien

This fully illustrated companion guide to *Your Body, Your Baby, Your Life* by Angela Phillips provides women with detailed exercises to help them through pregnancy and birth.

Working chronologically from the time when a woman may not even be pregnant but hopes to conceive in the near future right through to the birth itself, this accessible and clearly written guide gives women a comprehensive exercise programme for relaxation, combating morning sickness, stage fright in the last few weeks of pregnancy and for strengthening the pelvic floor muscles.

0 86358 047 5p   Handbook   Illustrated
0 86358 049 0c   160pp

WORKING YOUR WAY TO THE BOTTOM
The Feminization of Poverty

Hilda Scott

The 'new poor' of today are invisible.

They are also women.

It is a special kind of poverty, the causes of which are not fully understood by most men working in official and unofficial poverty research. Hilda Scott argues that they are blinded by assumptions about 'women's place' to the work that women actually do and the incomes they actually receive. For example, is a secretary considered working class if married to an assembly line worker but middle class if married to an accountant? And what happens if she is divorced from the accountant?

Hilda Scott produces startling evidence to prove that women the world over are rapidly becoming the 'new poor'. She argues that unless there is a radical re-think of economic policy women will keep on 'working their way to the bottom'.

0 86358 011 4p   192pp   General/
Contemporary political and economic issues

NAKED IS THE BEST DISGUISE
My Life as a Stripper

Lauri Lewin

A sensitive and provocative account of Lauri Lewin's life as a stripper in Boston. She describes how the stripping world operates and, using powerful narrative, provides many answers as to why it is that some women turn to stripping for a living.

'I recommend Lewin's *Naked is the Best Disguise* to all those who think that there is only one right answer – one correct angle of vision –

to the complex question of how we approach our own sexuality in the world.'

Alice Kessler Harris, *Women's Review*

'A book of honest observation and true memory, backed by feeling and intelligence. This is not a glib romanticization of the sex industry. Instead it is a woman's story, told with self respect and a lot of authentic regard for other women too.'

Andrea Dworkin

0 86358 077 7p   208pp   Autobiography

THE HEROIN USERS

Tam Stewart

By allowing the facts to speak for themselves, Tam Stewart disproves media-fuelled myths that all heroin users are irresponsible or inadequate; dispels the exaggerated notion of heroin, the 'devil-drug' from which there is no escape.

Based on the Liverpool drug scene of the last ten years and on interviews with addicts and doctors, the author tells the inside story of the heroin users. She traces the path of addiction, revealing the reasons for initial attraction to the drug; the experiences and suffering which increasing involvement causes; and investigates the possibility of a cure. A discussion of views held by doctors and law-makers sets the whole problem in context.

0 86358 111 0p   288pp
0 86358 088 2c   Social Questions

WOMEN'S SILENCE, MEN'S VIOLENCE
Sexual Assault in England, 1770–1845

Anna Clark

From the Yorkshire farm labourer who fought off her attacker for three hours, to the London servant forcibly seduced, this is a fascinating book.

Anna Clark's contribution to the growing literature on the historical perspective of sexual assault is unique in providing the vivid testimony of the victims themselves. She contrasts the words and experiences of these women with the patriarch practices and prejudices of the law courts and society officials, which masked the reality of male violence. She also recreates the bawdy world of eighteenth century London and the factories and moors of nineteenth century Yorkshire; the two areas of her research. This readable account gives us an historical context to one of today's most important feminist issues; resurrecting the voices of these angry but silenced women.

0 86358 103 Xp   192pp
History/Social Questions